D1565151

D^

Great Careers

Manufacturing and Transportation

with a High School Diploma

Titles in the *Great Careers* series

Great Careers

Manufacturing and Transportation

with a High School Diploma

Jessica Cohn

Ferguson Publishing
An imprint of Infobase Publishing

Great Careers with a High School Diploma
Manufacturing and Transportation

Copyright © 2008 by Infobase Publishing, Inc.

Ferguson
An imprint of Infobase Publishing
132 West 31st Street
New York, NY 10001

ISBN-13:978-0-8160-7050-3

Library of Congress Cataloging-in-Publication Data

Great careers with a high school diploma. — 1st ed.
    v. cm.
  Includes bibliographical references and index
  Contents: [1] Food, agriculture, and natural resources — [2] Construction and trades — [3] Communications, the arts, and computers —
[4] Sales, marketing, business, and finance — [5] Personal care services, fitness, and education — [6] Health care, medicine, and science —
[7] Hospitality, human services, and tourism — [8] Public safety, law, and security — [9] Manufacturing and transportation — [10] Armed forces.
  ISBN-13: 978-0-8160-7046-6 (v.1)
  ISBN-10: 0-8160-7046-6 (v.1)
  ISBN-13: 978-0-8160-7043-5 (v.2)
  ISBN-10: 0-8160-7043-1 (v.2)
[etc.]
1. Vocational guidance — United States. 2. Occupations — United States.
3. High school graduates — Employment — United States.
  HF5382.5.U5G677 2007
  331.702'330973 — dc22

                                                                2007029883

Ferguson books are available at special discounts when purchased in bulk quantities for businesses, associations, institutions, or sales promotions. Please call our Special Sales Department in New York at (212) 967-8800 or (800) 322-8755.

You can find Ferguson on the World Wide Web at
http://www.fergpubco.com

Produced by Print Matters, Inc.
Text design by A Good Thing, Inc.
Cover design by Salvatore Luongo

Printed in the United States of America

Sheridan PMI 10 9 8 7 6 5 4 3 2 1

This book is printed on acid-free paper.

Contents

Great Careers

How to Use This Book

This book, part of the Great Careers with a High School Diploma series, highlights in-demand careers that require no more than a high school diploma or the general educational development (GED) credential and offer opportunities for personal growth and professional advancement to motivated readers who are looking for a field that's right for them. The focus throughout is on the fastest-growing jobs with the best potential for advancement in the field. Readers learn about future prospects while discovering jobs they may never have heard of.

Knowledge—of yourself and about a potential career—is a powerful tool in launching yourself professionally. This book tells you how to use it to your advantage, explore job opportunities, and identify a good fit for yourself in the working world.

Each chapter provides the essential information needed to find not just a job but a career that draws on your particular skills and interests. All chapters include the following features:

- "Is This Job for You?" presents a set of questions for you to answer about yourself to help you learn if you have what it takes to work in a given career.
- "Let's Talk Money" and "Lets Talk Trends" provide at a glance crucial information about salary ranges and employment prospects.
- "What You'll Do" provides descriptions of the essentials of each job.
- "Where You'll Work" relates the details of the settings and the rules and patterns typical of that field.
- "Your Typical Day" provides details about what a day on the job involves for each occupation.
- "The Inside Scoop" presents firsthand information from someone working in the field.
- "What You Can Do Now" provides advice on getting prepared for your future career.
- "What Training You'll Need" discusses state requirements, certifications, and courses or other training you may need as you get started on your new career path.
- "How to Talk Like a Pro" defines a few key terms that give a feel for the occupation.

✴ "How to Find a Job" gives the practical how-tos of landing a position.

✴ "Secrets for Success" and "Reality Check" share inside information on getting ahead.

✴ "Some Other Jobs to Think About" lists similar related careers to consider.

✴ "How You Can Move Up" outlines how people in each occupation turn a job into a career, advancing in responsibility and earnings power.

✴ "Web Sites to Surf" lists Web addresses of trade organizations and other resources providing more information about the career.

In addition to a handy comprehensive index, the back of the book features an appendix providing invaluable information on job hunting strategies and techniques. This section provides general tips on interviewing, constructing a strong résumé, and gathering professional references. Use this book to discover a career that seems right for you—the tools to get you where you want to be are at your fingertips.

Introduction

No one has all the answers in life, and few people have things figured out by age 18. Yet answers are demanded of you as you end your high school career. One of the biggest decisions facing you, it seems, is what to do for a living. That choice affects everything. Yet knowing for certain which career path to follow is a rare occurrence among high school students. It just is.

Many high school students are mature and capable. But having positive answers about the best job and the right steps to take after high school—knowing for sure—that's something else again.

It is the job of your high school counselors to provide information about promising careers and the steps needed to get there. Counselors, teachers, and other professionals can help you analyze your strengths—and weaknesses—to figure out which jobs might be a good fit for you. There is plenty of information available about jobs that are in growth fields, including books like this one. But in the end, your career decisions are your own, and yours alone.

It's likely that you are already getting advice, some of it wanted and some of it not so welcome. You might be hearing that computers are the way to go—after all, jobs in this field are numerous and offer good salaries—yet not everyone feels attracted to this line of work. We might all need to use computer programs and the Internet, but we don't all want to be computer specialists. So what else is out there?

Plenty! The jobs most people know the most about are those done by the people in their social circles, especially parents, guardians, other relatives, and friends. But there are many other positions that need filling, and there are multiple paths you can take to get from high school to retirement.

Those paths twist and turn. No two people will follow the exact same career path any more than any two people are the same. You goal is to find work that matches your skills and personality—something that will keep you satisfied—and go from there.

Finding a good first job can seem daunting, but you *can* find it, you really can, and chances are it is a position you don't know much about at the moment. You may still have a year or two left to go in high school. Or you may be down to months or weeks to go. Either way, take some courage. People have been choosing and changing careers since history began. People have been graduating and making a go of life for many generations.

To that end, this book looks at a dozen specific jobs and what you can expect from them. At the very least, thinking about these jobs can lead you to some other ones.

School is Out—Now What?

This book is part of the series *Great Careers with a High School Diploma,* which is exactly what it says it is: A study of in-demand careers that can be started with a high-school diploma or a GED. This volume concentrates on careers in transportation and manufacturing, two very important fields that help drive the U.S. economy. Other books in the series look at other fields—from sales to construction.

You can use the books in this series to "try on" different jobs—to imagine yourself doing the work. You can read this book's chapter on being a taxi driver, for instance, and think about what your life would be like if driving were your profession. Or you can use the books in this series as reference material for specific career questions you may have. You can use this volume, for instance, to look up the kinds of courses you should be taking to become a chemical technician.

All the jobs under consideration are available to a high school graduate, and there is a very practical reason for this focus. For millions of Americans, life after high school does not mean another four years in a protective school environment. It means stepping into the real world. Each year, more than 900,000 of the nation's 2.8 million high school graduates go directly into the workforce.

College isn't immediately in the cards for everyone, for a number of reasons. Some people learn best by using their hands rather than by sitting in a classroom, so they are aching to get out and work. Others find that college costs, which get higher all the time, are well beyond reach their reach, at least for the immediate future.

Tuition and fees at a four-year public college averaged $5,491 during the 2005–2006 school year, according to the College Board. That's a huge hunk of change, and that average does not include housing costs. It's a simple fact of life that not everyone can meet those fiscal demands upon high school graduation.

Happily, a number of satisfying careers are available without a four-year bachelor's degree or even a two-year associate's degree. These jobs span a wide range and can serve as a first step or provide lifetime satisfaction. So what careers are available? The range is so broad that *Great Careers with a High School Diploma* includes 10 volumes, each based on related career fields from the Department of Labor's career clusters. Graduates can find work as apprentice electronics technician and chefs. They become teacher's assistant and Web page designers. They work as sales associates and lab technicians. And that's just the start.

Each volume profiles at least 10 careers, encouraging readers to focus on a wide selection of job possibilities. Some of these are positions that relatively few people know much about. To enable readers to narrow their choices, each chapter offers a self-assessment quiz that helps answer this question: "Is this career for me?" What's more, each job profile includes a look at what the position involves, highlights of a typical day, insight into the work environment, and an interview with someone on the job. That's when you get to hear, in a unique and individual voice, what these careers are like.

Doing Your Homework

Wherever you work, whatever you do, it is wise to undergo additional training as time goes on, so you can move up. But in some of these positions, that training can be found on the job, through a certificate program, or during an apprenticeship, which combines entry-level work and class time. A number of good employers are anxious to help their employees with educational assistance, by providing either classes or money for tuition. They know that helping people get ahead is a good way to build loyalty.

Great Careers features opportunities that require no further academic study or training beyond high school as well as those that do. For most of the featured positions, you can start prepping while in high school through related volunteer work and internships. You can take academic classes, join technical programs, or attend career academies, as many do. For each job being profiled in this series, the best ways to prepare are featured in a "What You Can Do Now" section.

For those readers who are called to the Armed Forces, the decision to serve the country can also provide these kinds of training opportunities. Every branch of the Armed Forces, from the Army to the Coast Guard, offers job training. These programs include administration, construction, electronics, health care, and protective services. In fact, one volume of Great Careers with a High School Diploma is devoted to careers that come from military training. Related jobs range from personnel specialist to aircraft mechanic.

Take It by Sections

Each chapter looks at one job and brings up several related careers to help you sort through your thoughts about the work. Each chapter also talks about ways to advance in the field. "How to Get Hired," yet another section in each chapter, provides job hunting tips specific to each career. So, for instance, advice for train track maintenance workers includes a tip on taking shop in school. Some of these tips, such as reading up on industry news, apply across the board. You see, employers of entry-level workers aren't looking for degrees and academic achievements. They want employability skills: A sense of responsibility, a willingness to learn, discipline, flexibility, and above all enthusiasm. Luckily, with 100 jobs profiled in Great Careers with a High School Diploma, finding the perfect one to get enthusiastic about is easier than ever.

Ways to Go in Transportation

The jobs featured in the first nine chapters are all about transportation. The transportation field includes everything from highway construction to passenger car rental, from ship building to bus driving. In 2006, the U.S. transportation sector accounted for $1.4 trillion. The sector employs 16 percent of all workers and makes up a bit more than 10 percent of U.S. economic activity, according to Plunkett Research.

The volume of supplies being moved from place to place is expected to increase 70 percent, as measured from 1998 to 2020, says the U.S. Department of Transportation. So there will not be a lack of related jobs anytime soon. Land, air, and sea vehicles need to be driven, built, and maintained, as do roads and rails. Besides offering a base of employment, the transportation field provides people with plenty of personal satisfaction.

Many of these jobs are union jobs, with good benefits. In a number of these positions, you would be supervised yet in charge of your own time throughout the day.

Building a Future in Manufacturing

The manufacturing jobs featured in the final three chapters are those of equipment operator, machinist, and chemical technician, important roles in the national economy. These job titles can be found in many categories of business, from environmental engineering to food science.

Equipment operators run the machines that make what we need. They perform basic manufacturing and construction tasks with precision. They are on the frontlines of the economy, as are machinists. Machinists provide the tools on which everything else is built. When a new manufacturing step is introduced, they are called on for creative solutions, inventing new forms for the process.

Technicians are frontline workers too, working in labs rather than outdoors or on production floors. The role of a chemical technician, which is addressed in this volume, is meant to be representational of the tech field. Technicians, working in specialties such as quality control, and in most industries you can think of, help theory work in the real world. The great pluses of these fields is that your supervisors recognize the need for continuing training that will help you expand your knowledge base. So you're not likely to stagnate.

Making It Pay

Great Careers covers jobs that have been undergoing growth, which tends to be fastest among the positions that call for additional tech training or a certificate of proficiency. The chief economist at the Economic Policy Foundation, a think tank, has said that there are more of these positions available than there are workers to fill them. In fact, only 23 percent of the jobs available in the coming years will require a four-year degree or higher, the foundation reports.

It's often said that higher education is linked to higher earnings, and while this is often the case, it is not the whole story. The gap that exists between the wages of high school graduates and those with college degrees has started to close, if slightly. Between 2000 and 2004, the Economic Policy Foundation found, the yearly earnings of college graduates dropped by 5.6 percent while the earnings of high school graduates increased modestly by 1.6 percent. High school graduates earn a median yearly income of $26,104, according the U.S. Census Bureau.

Meanwhile, some 43 percent of four-year grads are underemployed. That is to say, they may have earned degrees in political science and ended up waiting tables. Having every opportunity made available to you is not always fruitful. If you've invested six years and tens of thousands of dollars into a law school education, only to discover you dislike the profession, there's nowhere to go for a refund.

Many people, instead of following a four- or six-year educational path, take their advancement in steps, by getting work, making adjustments, and adding education as needed. Of course, paying for even a certificate or one-year degree can seem to be beyond your means at first. But financial aid is not just for four-year college students—those attending trade, technical, vocational, two-year, and career colleges can also qualify for aid. For instance, SallieMae (http://www.salliemae.com) offers very specific private loans for career training, and U.S. Bank just introduced the CampUS Education Loan specifically for those attending two-year schools. Just be careful, if you take out loans, to consider what your monthly repayment amount would be, and weigh that against your prospective monthly earnings.

Workers with a certificate or one-year degree can continue their education—and can often transfer credits earned. Even someone who performed below average in high school can excel afterward if he or she puts in the time and energy.

Finding Your Way

So which job sounds right as a starting point? Consider some interesting jobs in transportation and manufacturing and see how they are intertwined. The chemical technician tests the paint that the truck driver delivers to distribution centers. In fact, all the books and jobs in the series are related. After all, we all need one another.

If you like what you read about one job, you might also consider the related careers listed at the end of that chapter. There may be something there for you to study further. All lists are meant as a starting point for your personalized job search. One thing leads to another.

Just be sure to consider the needed skill sets and abilities and the future prospects of each position. The more you know about any given job, the better you will be able to make a decision about your probability of success doing the work. The very first chapter, for example, is about becoming an automotive technician. So can you picture yourself doing that kind of work? Do you even know what to picture? That job is the perfect example of work that is typically misunderstood. These days, fixing cars has a lot to do with computers. To find out why, read on.

Master auto electronics and engines

Auto Technician (Auto, Body, Glass, and Specialty Technician)

Rev up your career by learning auto repair

Help keep the nation's drivers road-ready

Auto Technician (Auto, Body, Glass, and Specialty Technician)

When your car is making funny noises, you call a shop where some-one can diagnose the problem and get you on your way. These experts in car engine repair used to be known as "auto mechanics." But now they are called "auto technicians" to reflect what's going on in-side modern engines. These days complex computers and electronics run vehicles, and employers are looking for individuals who can han-dle these new technologies. Lucky you if you're one of them because a career as an auto tech is a smart way to go! Around 35,000 jobs related to automobile technology will open each year through 2010, according to the U.S. Bureau of Labor Statistics. This job surplus, say experts, is due in part to the misperception that working with cars is a dirty job—which is just not true!

Is This Job for You?

Would you make a good auto technician? To find out, read each of the following questions, and answer "Yes" or "No."

Yes	No	**1.**	Do you like to solve problems?
Yes	No	**2.**	Do you enjoy working with your hands?
Yes	No	**3.**	Can you approach things logically?
Yes	No	**4.**	Are you comfortable working with hand tools?
Yes	No	**5.**	Are you good at communicating?
Yes	No	**6.**	Are you comfortable around computerized shop equipment?
Yes	No	**7.**	Do you understand the importance of a checklist?
Yes	No	**8.**	Do you have the agility needed to work under raised cars?
Yes	No	**9.**	Do you work well with people?
Yes	No	**10.**	Do you like cars?

If you said "Yes" to most of these questions, becoming an auto technician might be a good avenue to explore. To find out more about this career, read on.

Let's Talk Money

Entry-level jobs in the field pay from $24,000 to $41,000 per year, according to 2007 figures from Salary Wizard. But a salary range of $37,000 to $60,000 is the norm once you have some experience. Median earnings in 2006 were almost $16.92 an hour, according to the U.S. Bureau of Labor Statistics, or $35,194 a year.

What You'll Do

Working with autos is growing less mechanical and more technical all the time. Open the hood of a new vehicle, and what you see are integrated electronic systems and computers. As a technician, you'll understand how these interior components work together, so you can diagnose and repair problems. If you are working in a repair shop, the owner of the vehicle will give you a description of the problem as a starting point. You'll then use diagnostic tools that read the vehicle's performance levels, test whether systems are in working order, and highlight trouble spots. You'll utilize onboard diagnostic computers and gauges, and you'll employ handheld diagnostic computers as well.

Figuring out the root of the problem is often a process of elimination. The "ping" an owner is hearing when he or she drives could be nothing more than a loose screw on the dashboard. Or it could be symptomatic of something serious. Once you have located the real problem, you'll refer to related engineering materials to figure out how to proceed. On one hand, you'll be using sophisticated computerized equipment to fix the problem. On the other, you'll be utilizing classic hand and power tools for repair—from wrenches to jacks to welding equipment.

If you are working in a maintenance shop, you will be called upon to perform safety checks and make refills, such as lubricating engines and changing filters. Your goal is to keep vehicles operating safely and their owners' troubles to a minimum. For this line of service, you need to enjoy being helpful. You should like to fix problems. Then you will enjoy the satisfaction of a job well done.

Who You'll Work For

- ✮ Auto dealers
- ✮ Auto parts retailers and suppliers
- ✮ Auto rental and leasing companies
- ✮ Body work shops
- ✮ Company fleets
- ✮ Federal, state, and local government garages
- ✮ Gas station repair shops
- ✮ High school and community college shops
- ✮ Oil change chains
- ✮ Private repair shops
- ✮ State inspection stations
- ✮ Taxi companies
- ✮ Transmission shops
- ✮ Tune-up shops

Where You'll Work

Let's say you manage an oil-change shop. Your day includes interacting with all kinds of people, from high school kids trying to maintain their first cars to busy executives dropping off their vehicles before work. Maintenance technicians often look out over busy streets through large glass-paneled doors. They move from pit to platform and often trade duties with associates partway through the day.

Most techs are employed at bright, clean auto dealerships and private shops, where they're given a roster of duties for the day. You will work in high-ceilinged rooms filled with other techs, your equipment,

Let's Talk Trends

Through 2014, demand for new technicians is expected to grow steadily, according to the Bureau of Labor Statistics. Consider what's happening: More vehicles are taking to the roads as the number of multi-car families continues to increase. Meanwhile, many technicians are planning to retire soon. Auto dealers and independent repair shops foresee plentiful openings.

The Inside Scoop: Q&A

Noemi Castro
Service technician
Cerritos, California

Q: *How did you get your job?*

A: I just moved to the greater Los Angeles area. To get work, I just started applying at different dealerships. I didn't read about my job in the newspaper or anything. I just asked about work and got it. I had some experience with CAP [College Automotive Program]. It's the specific school for Chrysler manufacturers. Before that, I was a tech trainee for almost three years through AYES [Automotive Youth Education Service] at my local high school. They had what was called job shadowing.

Q: *What do you like best about your job?*

A: The best thing about the job is there's so much variety, and it's very challenging—especially with all the newer vehicles. The electrical components don't really change, but they keep getting updated. It's not just the same thing over and over again.

Q: *What's the most challenging thing about your job?*

A: There aren't very many women in the field. The most challenging part is when you first start—it's male dominated. So I just show up to work and keep at it. I'm very thankful that the service technicians are very open-minded. They can see me as someone who just wants to do a good job.

Q: *What are the keys to success to being an automobile technician?*

A: Most of all is persistence! I definitely think persistence is important—that and honesty, of course. You have to be very honest. It's also very logical [work]. You have to think outside the box sometimes. You have to be very open-minded as far as the problem goes. You can't just say, "Well, this is what fixed it last time." You have to follow the steps and take a new approach.

and a line of vehicles that have been hauled in for service. You'll move with ease among the diagnostic equipment in your "corner" and the other departments, such as parts.

Techs often work more than 40 hours a week, with some evening and weekend work. Shop owners are usually careful to make certain the areas are well-lit and ventilated. There are exceptions, of course, but you can probably avoid them. At the other end of the spectrum, there's the ultimate glamour spot of a NASCAR or Formula One pit— the elaborately decorated racetrack slots where superbly well-coordinated crews of experience-ripened professionals give cars makeovers in the time it takes a light to change.

Your Typical Day

Here are what your duties might be in a typical day.

✓ **Settle in.** Look over the vehicles and tasks on your scheduled "to do" list, and decide a course of action, based on what has been promised to the customers, which parts are available, and how long each task will take.

✓ **Diagnose problems.** Using a checklist and diagnostic tools, you examine a troubled vehicle. You confer with your fellow techs and managers. People will provide anecdotes about similar repairs they have done. Still, you allow each case its independent evaluation.

✓ **Perform the repair or maintenance.** You use hand and power tools as needed for smooth and safe continued operation of the vehicle, you also provide recommendations for further service, if you notice that a part is on its last legs.

What You Can Do Now

✴ Take advantage of related vocational courses, such as electronics, in high school. Math and science courses will help you with the basic principles.

✴ Find an apprenticeship or a training program, such as an Automotive Youth Education Service (AYES) program, offered through 500 or schools and more than 4,000 dealerships. And start building your tool set.

✴ Find out about local trade schools that offer Automotive Service Excellence (ASE) certification, the minimum required by most employers. ASE certifications are offered in dozens of specialties; employers like to see these proofs of knowledge, especially when combined with substantive hands-on experience.

What Training You'll Need

Taking a job as a parts runner, who picks up parts at distributors and delivers them, or as a service writer, who writes up work orders can be your way in. Many large employers offer training programs for entry-level auto technicians, so choose your place of employment carefully.

Look for evening courses in auto repair while in high school. If you are lucky, your school may provide adequate training for a job as a technician's helper. Some schools are part of the AYES program, which will make you AYES-certified. If you have gone through that hoop, you will be attractive to employers. If these organized programs are not available where you live, just remember, anything you do to add to your training will help.

Earn your ASE certification through a night program, a shop-based program, or through a technical school or community college. With that, you can begin doing mechanical work. To work as a technician you'll need additional instruction and hands-on training with the kind of equipment you'll use on the job. The best of these schools have partnerships with employers, which will help you. The Accrediting Commission of Career Schools and Colleges of Technology certifies some of the schools. Just make sure that whatever program you choose, the technology is up-to-date.

The best of prospective employers offer opportunities for your professional development and continued training and certification. Look for a place of employment that gives those kinds of chances. You'll want to build a résumé of certifications and experience with computerized diagnostic systems. Keep in mind, as well, that you will want to build your own personal set of tools. As an automobile technician, your tools will become incredibly important to you!

How to Talk Like a Pro

Here are a few key words and phrases you'll hear as an auto technician:

⭐ **Alternative fuel vehicles** These are vehicles powered by something other than petroleum products: By water dehydrogenization, electric fuel cells, solar power, and the like. You'll need to understand the basic science behind these.

✯ **ASE certification** Recognition of a training program by the Institute for Automotive Service Excellence. ASE certification assures that a program meets standards and is regularly reviewed for excellence.

✯ **Hand tools** As an auto technician, hand tools are precious possessions. You will most likely be expected to provide your own on the job; having better tools will only make your day easier.

How to Find a Job

Follow the steps in "What Training You'll Need," making the most of every opportunity. Use the contacts you make while in high school jobs to meet employers who need your skills after graduation. Ask whether teachers and administrators at your training center can provide introductions. Any prospective employer is going to be interested in knowing what kinds of work you can already perform and what types of certifications you already have under your belt. Make that step easier by listing your accomplishments on a clear and engaging résumé. Have someone who knows your job history check your list to make sure everything important is on there.

Be prompt for any interviews, and show up rested and well-dressed. Communicate your dependability, resourcefulness, and people skills. Be willing to take on-the-job training and be happy for the opportunity to receive additional certifications through your employer. The more certifications you have, the higher hourly rate you may expect.

Secrets for Success

See the suggestions below and turn to the appendix for advice on résumés and interviews.

✯ You will sometimes have to twist yourself into a pretzel to get at the part of the engine where you belong. Stay in shape so that all that lifting of tools and parts—and yourself!—is not a problem.

✯ Remember—increasingly, techs are specializing. You might become the transmission genius. Or maybe you will be recognized as the air-conditioning specialist.

Reality Check

The job of an automotive technician can be stressful. You are dealing with breakdowns and problems, and your customers are not always in the best frame of mind. So take pride in being a people person. Know that someone's bad mood does not have to affect you.

Some Other Jobs to Think About

* Automotive-repair service estimator. Insurance companies need knowledgeable automotive people to check out accidents and damage to vehicles as part of the claims process. If you like to be out and about during the day, this might be the path for you.
* Shop supervisor or service manager. With leadership ability, you can plan to move up the ranks and run the shop day to day.
* Motorcycle or marine technician. Autos aren't the only vehicles with engines!

How You Can Move Up

* Follow advancements in technology and stay on top of your training efforts for the best shot at advancement in your shop—and the highest possible wage. If your dream is to own your own shop, learn all the aspects of the process, from operating all the machinery to dealing with people.
* Jump at opportunities to take responsibility and be at the ready with good ideas or a helping hand. If your plan includes course-work, consider a class in customer relations or stress management, to go along with any technical studies. However you do it, develop your communications skills.

Web Sites to Surf

Automotive Youth Educational Systems (AYES). Here is where you will find what you need to know about training programs sponsored by automotive manufacturers—and possibly your next step! http://www.ayes.org

National Institute for Automotive Service Excellence (ASE). Everything you need to know about becoming certified in the field is mentioned here, at least as a start. http://www.iatn.net/ase

Help keep the economy moving

Truck Driver

Learn how to service and drive a truck

Start a career that goes the distance

Truck Driver

It's hard to imagine just how tough life would get if truck drivers stopped doing what they do. There are more than 3 million drivers on the roads, moving everything from pickles and olives to computers. If they no longer did their jobs, grocery stores would empty, gas stations would run dry, businesses would stop running. The economy relies on the trucking industry to stay strong, and truckers are the heart of that effort. Some drivers deliver bread to local stores. Others move households. Yet others fill big box stores with everything from black socks to bubble gum. Loads are light or heavy, local or long distance. Some drivers are also involved in customer service, as representatives for the companies that employ them.

Is This Job for You?

Would driving a truck be a good career fit for you? To find out, read each of the following questions, and answer "Yes" or "No."

Yes	No	**1.**	Do you like to drive?
Yes	No	**2.**	Are you physically fit and capable of loading items?
Yes	No	**3.**	Do you have mental stamina (e.g., you can stay alert for prolonged periods)?
Yes	No	**4.**	Are you comfortable with the idea of driving at night?
Yes	No	**5.**	Do you have—and plan to keep—a clean driving record?
Yes	No	**6.**	Can you deal well with the public, including angry drivers?
Yes	No	**7.**	Are you free from diabetes, epilepsy, and color-blindness?
Yes	No	**8.**	Do you avoid the use of drugs and alcohol?
Yes	No	**9.**	Are you safety-minded?
Yes	No	**10.**	Can you navigate roads well?

If you answered yes to most of these questions, the career of a truck driver may be a good fit for you. To find out more about trucking, read on.

Let's Talk Money

The range of salaries for truck drivers differs by the type of truck driven. Light truck drivers earn the least—their median hourly salary is $12.17, or $25,314 a year, according to 2006 data from the U.S. Bureau of Labor Statistics. Tractor-trailer truck drivers earn more, on average; $16.85 is the median hourly wage, or $35,048 a year. Overall, however, median salary ranged $28,000 to $52,000 a year based on 2007 Salary Wizard data.

What You'll Do

A local driver is going to deliver goods, say, packages and messages, within set boundaries and start and end the day at a garage. But a long-distance driver at a carrier for hire might log a year of assignments that take him or her all over the country. Some aspects of the work are the same no matter what routes you take, however. To a greater or lesser extent, you are responsible for the fuel and oil and general safety of your truck. You'll check windshield wipers, mirrors, and lights. You'll make sure the fire extinguisher is working. You'll also be responsible for making sure the cargo is packed securely, though many larger outfits have separate departments handling most aspects of packing. After departure, your main job is staying alert and driving safely.

Any day can be a huge challenge in that regard because you just do not know what—or whom—you will meet on the road. You have to know how to keep your cool during long hours in a cab. You'll never control traffic, after all.

Getting items to their destinations safely and on time is job one. To help you along the way, you will probably be in radio or cell contact with the distribution center. Many trucking outfits have logicians working for them, helping the truckers anticipate road delays and other kinds of snares. You might be linked to your base with a GPS (Global Positioning System) unit, which uses satellite signals to keep track of your location and activity on the roads along the way. Some companies also monitor the fuel consumption and engine performance this way. You might work with another driver in a buddy system that allows you to progress to your destination almost continuously.

Who You'll Work For

✳ Distribution centers
✳ For-hire freight services
✳ Government agencies
✳ Local businesses
✳ Long-distance carriers
✳ Moving companies
✳ Restaurants
✳ Service providers, such as laundry services

Where You'll Work

Long-haul truck drivers will tell you that their office is the open road. But as a starting driver, you'll probably be tethered to some kind of distribution center, large or small. You might work for a stone-and-ceramic company, carrying newly manufactured tiles to retail distribution centers, where they will be loaded on yet another truck for their specific destination. You might work for a clothing designer and carry expensive togs to small boutiques in a large city. You could find yourself at a package delivery service, covering ground services in a county-wide area. Your route might be specific and change little over long periods of time. Or it might never duplicate itself. It all depends on your employer.

The trucks you might drive can be any of many sizes. Some drivers run vans and small trucks on daily runs. In that case, you'll load up and take care of a route, unloading goods at your destinations and probably tracking your work electronically. You might spend some time in the offices of your customers along the way, checking on the quality of services that they receive from your company.

Let's Talk Trends

Wage and salaried positions in trucking will grow in-line with the average for all other occupations through 2014, according to the Bureau of Labor Statistics. Opportunities will vary depending on that state of the economy, but stable industries, such as grocery stores, will be relatively unaffected by any unexpected downturns.

Those drivers who are responsible for heavy trucks or tractor-trailers usually stick to the highways. Some cover very long distances over several days. The route may change with each assignment, or you could have what is known as a dedicated run, a regular route. The cabs of these larger trucks can be rather elaborate, with sleeping berths. Truckers personalize their cabs; many take great pride in their roadway setups.

Your Typical Day

Here are a few highlights from a regular day out on the road.

✔ **Take a morning drive.** You are taking new cars from a plant in Michigan to dealerships in Pennsylvania. After a good lunch at a truck stop on the interstate, you call your dispatcher and report on your progress.

✔ **Listen up.** The dispatcher tells you that there's an overturned semi on the upcoming highway. You've already heard this, but you take her instructions for a way you can avoid that stretch of road.

✔ **Take a load off.** After arriving at your first stop, you park on a service road and find out who will be taking the cars to their spots. You do the unloading, because the ramps are tricky.

What You Can Do Now

✯ Keep your driving record clean. Stay out of trouble with the law.

✯ To drive within most states, you just need to be 18. But to drive a commercial vehicle between states, you must be 21, and some firms require that you be older than that. You can take driver training and auto mechanics in preparation.

✯ Research driving schools in your area. The Professional Truck Driver Institute certifies training centers.

What Training You'll Need

This field is regulated by state and federal governments. If you expect to drive a truck weighing more than 26,000 pounds, or a truck of any size that carries hazardous materials, you need a commercial driver's license (CDL). Some exceptions can be made for firefighters, the military, and similar personnel, but you should get a commercial license.

The Inside Scoop: Q&A

Dora Colvin
Long-distance driver
Joplin, Missouri

Q: *How did you get your job?*

A: I was raised on a farm in North Dakota, and I married a guy who drove a truck from Texas. Now, I drove everything there was on the farm . . . but as kids came along, I taught school. I was a bookkeeper for a while. And when the kids went to college and the dog died, I went on the road with [my husband].

Q: *What do you like best about your job?*

A: It's wonderful. You see all of America's beauty, and each state has its own. It's that and the people you meet. We have the most fun. Being on a dedicated run [from Tennessee to Washington state], you get to know the people in the area.

Q: *What's the most challenging part of your job?*

A: Home time is the challenge in long-haul trucking. We have a sweet deal. We get to have dinner with our grandchildren on Tuesdays on the way out. But that doesn't happen for most people. Scheduling the down time to be with family can be a challenge.

Q: *What are the keys to success to being a truck driver?*

A: Attitude! You've got to enjoy what you're doing. There's no question. I've had four career changes, and I've loved them all. It's how you look at it and how you apply yourself. You have to go in there and do the best you can.

Each state offers it, and information on obtaining one can be found through your state department of motor vehicle offices. Basically, you'll have to pass a background check and pass written and road tests. The states check with one another; if you lose your license in one, it will not be renewed in another.

When you get a CDL, you surrender all your other licenses. You will be tested every couple of years and must continue to pass a physical to hold on to the CDL. The doctors want to make sure you have at least 20/40 vision. That can be corrected with eyeglasses or contacts, but you must be able to see at least that well. You must also have a 70 degree field of vision. You must be able to hear a whisper from five feet away. That can include the use of a hearing aid. You must have what is considered normal use of hands and arms and have normal blood pressure, which can include controlling it by taking a prescribed medicine. You must be able to see all colors and cannot be issued a license if you have epilepsy or diabetes. In order to carry hazardous material, you'll also need to pass with the U.S. Department of Homeland Security's Transportation Security Administration, which will run a criminal background check on you and collect your fingerprints.

The standards above are the minimum. Some employers will also test to make sure you can lift and carry loads. Others will require that you have already driven for a number of years. Still others require a yearly physical exam. A number of employers test for drug and alcohol use as well.

How to Talk Like a Pro

Here are a few terms you may hear as a truck driver:

- ✦ **International Brotherhood of Teamsters** Most truck drivers belong to this union.
- ✦ **Air, hydraulic, and antilock (ABS) braking systems** You'll need to know basic truck maintenance, so you can keep your rig in working order.
- ✦ **U.S. Department of Transportation** This government department sets many of the rules you need to follow as a driver.

How to Find a Job

As you leave high school, you may not yet be old enough for a commercial license, but you can plan ahead. Employers like drivers who know the basics of truck maintenance. So you can take classes that teach you about the electrical systems, the drivetrain, the brakes, the steering and suspension systems, and more. People who know basic refrigeration will be attractive to employers of refrigeration trucks.

Find out your state requirements for your CDL and follow through on the steps you need to take. Stay in shape and look for openings in Web postings, the newspaper classifieds, and at government employment agencies. Show up to your interview on time and show your knowledge of trucking. Be respectful when you ask for work.

Secrets for Success

See the suggestions below and turn to the appendix for advice on résumés and interviews.

* Companies want to hire drivers who are: responsible, efficient, and relatively cheap to insure. You will hit a home run on all three counts if you take professional driving courses.
* Exercise courtesy in your driving and in your contacts with customers and other people you encounter while working. No one likes to pay a hothead to take the wheel, and your decency will make for more pleasant days.

Reality Check

Driving trucks is not always a 9-to-5 job. You might be asked to drive overnights and spend time clocking hours on lonely highways.

Some Other Jobs to Think About

* Bus driver. Like truck drivers, bus drivers are responsible for moving huge pieces of machinery safely; however, this job involves constant contact with the public.
* Dispatcher. If you like the trucking industry but are not wild about clocking so many hours on the road, you can look for work that supports drivers, such as working as a dispatcher.
* Taxi and limo driver. If you like to drive, and you expertly know your way around a metropolitan center, this is another way to go. Here too, a genial disposition helps.

How You Can Move Up

* Aim to be a long-distance trucker. This specialty generally pays more than other kinds of driving.
* Volunteer a bit of time to help at one of the related professional organizations, such as United Highway Carriers Association. In

any case, you can work your way up if you stay abreast of trucking issues.

✦ Jump to take on different responsibilities and assignments. You'll get a sense of all the challenges of the work and you can become a better supervisor.

✦ Strive to buy your own truck and become your own boss.

Web Sites to Surf

American Trucking Associations, Inc. At this site, you will find information on job openings and issues related to the industry.
http://www.truckline.com

Professional Truck Driver Institute. Before you take related classes, make sure the instructors are working for a certified school. Check with this site. http://www.ptdi.org

Enjoy a career on the road

Bus Driver

Get behind the wheel to get your future in gear

Be part of the transportation industry

Bus Driver

In rural, suburban, and urban settings, professional bus drivers are needed to get people where they need to be. The work is straightforward—you pick up and drop off passengers on a schedule—but assignments vary. Local transit drivers take commuters to and from work and shopping venues. Intercity drivers take passengers on sightseeing tours. These days, there are more than 650,000 drivers on the roads, according to 2006 data from the U.S. Bureau of Labor Statistics. More than 70 percent are school bus drivers. Still, bus drivers of all kinds are needed to manage groups of people with ease—and to maneuver large vehicles over streets and highways.

Is This Job for You?

Would working as a bus driver be a good fit for you? To find out, read each of the following questions, and answer "Yes" or "No."

Yes	No	**1.**	Do you communicate with people easily?
Yes	No	**2.**	Do you have a helpful manner?
Yes	No	**3.**	Would you be comfortable driving a large vehicle?
Yes	No	**4.**	Do you have a clean record so you can get a commercial vehicle license?
Yes	No	**5.**	Do you understand or can you learn basic motor mechanics?
Yes	No	**6.**	Are you responsible and dependable?
Yes	No	**7.**	Could you deal with the many personalities on the bus?
Yes	No	**8.**	Can you stay alert in all kinds of weather and at all times of day?
Yes	No	**9.**	Can you work well without direct supervision?
Yes	No	**10.**	Do you stand up well to fatigue?

If you answered "Yes" to most of these questions, you may have what it takes to pursue a career as a bus driver. To find out more about this job, read on.

What You'll Do

No matter what kind of route you have, your main job is customer service. Whether you transport schoolkids or sightseers, you have to

Let's Talk Money

Bus drivers, full- and part-time, earned approximately $15,000 to $26,000 annually, with bonuses, in 2007. School bus drivers earned $21,000 to $39,000 in that same time frame, according to Salary Wizard. Median hourly salary, according to the U.S. Bureau of Labor Statistics, was about $12 in 2006 (or $25,000 a year), while transit and intercity drivers earned a median hourly wage of $15.43 (about $32,000 per year).

stay courteous, alert, and helpful. The people you carry can be fine one moment and crabby the next, so as a driver, you need to stay even-tempered. A sense of humor helps.

In most instances, you'll have a set course to follow. City driving requires plenty of stop-and-go action; rural routes, less so. But in either case, your main concern is the safety of the passengers. You will do your best to make their ride smooth and, quite frankly, uneventful. You'll be driving your bus in all kinds of weather, so some days will present special challenges.

School bus drivers deliver students to their school and their homes. The work sometimes involves discipline and crowd management. You will be asked to drive groups of students for field trips and athletic events. You have to stay tuned to the mood of the crowd and anticipate and head off problems. Drivers in charge of local and intercity routes will collect fares. Throughout the day, you'll answer questions about routes and transfers. You might make several loops over the same area within a day. Or you may have a route that connects towns and cities along a highway, making one, longer, one-way trip. Many drivers are required to fill out daily logs of where they traveled and what problems, if any, they encountered along the way. If there's a mechanical issue, you may be expected to repair it or have it repaired. At the very least, you will be asked to report relevant details. Drivers who take passengers across state lines have to report the distances they traveled and the hours they devoted to driving and downtime.

Who You'll Work For

★ Charter services
★ Ground passenger transport services

Let's Talk Trends

Current drivers tend to be older—and will be retiring, which means younger drivers will have opportunities to step into driver positions. Industry insiders say potential drivers will find job openings in the foreseeable future, with the government predicting employment to increase as fast as average.

✴ Individual and family social service organizations
✴ Intercity bus lines
✴ Local government
✴ Municipal bus systems
✴ Private schools, both day schools and boarding schools
✴ Public school systems

Where You'll Work

You might ferry preschool children or students with special needs in smaller buses that are more like large vans. Your small or large bus could be brand-new or ancient, quiet or loud. Opportunities in municipal bus systems vary widely as well. You could be driving an old diesel vehicle or a clean-air hybrid, just off the assembly line. Some cities and counties have a web of public transport involving large and small buses. So you might have a route that helps workers getting to and from their cross-city jobs. Or you might drive a smaller bus that carries suburbanites into and back from an urban environment. Some drivers transport senior citizens to special services. Others specialize in moving troubled children to and from appointments. You might drive an interstate bus that carries people who want to visit far-flung relatives or see another part of the world. Or you might take charters, delivering people to recreation spots or special competitions or conferences. Some of these vehicles are state-of-the-art, with ample room, entertainment systems, and advanced air-conditioning systems. You'll be spending a good part of your time in the driver's seat in the cab, where it's usually comfortable enough. But you'll put in long hours sitting and waiting, in your cab and at your customers'

The Inside Scoop: Q&A

James Britton
Motor coach operator
Millersville, Maryland

Q: *How did you get your job?*

A: Bus driving was something I wanted to do since I was a kid. I used to sit up front all the time with the Greyhound bus driver. My mom would take me out of town all the time. Basically, if you've got a permit and a clean record, you can do this. I did my training for about a month. I did my road test, and that was that. But a bus is big, remember. Some people say, "OK, I'd like to drive a bus," and they try it, but they get into it and find out it's not for them.

Q: *What do you like best about your job?*

A: It's a job where no one is looking over your shoulder but the customer. You're kind of like captain of the ship. If you want to take a break, you work it out with the customer. You get to go to different places and get paid for it. You go to different places and meet different people. I've been all over the place. It's good to get out. It opens your mind up.

Q: *What's the most challenging part of your job?*

A: The most challenging part is safety: Being safe, operating your vehicle in a safe manner, protecting the people on the bus and the people around you—because any moment anything can happen. You've got a lot of people around with bad driving habits.

Q: *What are the keys to success to being a bus driver?*

A: You have to be a responsible individual, and you have to have patience, and you have to have morals and a careful life. You're carrying people's grandmothers and people's mothers. Sometimes I'm carrying a busload of kids. Someone who can make a difference in the world might be on my bus.

destinations—while your passengers take in the sights. During the busy season, you will log plenty of overnights, often falling into bed at 10 p.m. or so at night.

Your Typical Day

Here are highlights of a typical day for a charter bus driver.

- ✓ **Make a safety check.** You look over the bus and make certain that everything is clean and ready to go. You check the tires, brakes, and windshield wipers. You make sure the gas, oil, and water are OK. You go down a checklist, which includes making sure the fire extinguishers and first aid kits are aboard.
- ✓ **Meet and greet your group.** Help your passengers check their luggage and board. Explain the safety and comfort features of the bus. Show them entertainment items, such as the video player.
- ✓ **Move that bus!** When everyone is settled in, you take off on the first leg of your adventure. You maneuver through city streets, and then settle into the lull of highway driving.

What You Can Do Now

- ✗ Keep a clean driving record. Practice safe driving.
- ✗ Do volunteer work that helps you understand social service and what it's like to deal with many kinds of people.
- ✗ Research the behind-the-wheel and classroom training given by intercity bus companies and transit systems nearby. If you hope to be a school bus driver, find out what the district and state require for your CDL (commercial driver's license).

What Training You'll Need

To earn a CDL, you basically surrender your other licenses. You have to have a clean driving record to do so. You also need to earn a "passenger" endorsement. That means you have to pass tests of your related knowledge and skills, such as being able to memorize routes. Different bus companies and systems have their own training programs to get you to that point, but they follow a basic formula. You will be given two to eight weeks of classroom instruction and behind-the-wheel training. Most people who learn to drive a bus never tried to drive anything that large until they went into training, so most potential drivers start off with the same amount of experience.

Before you're given the keys and a job, you'll practice moving the bus through various courses. You'll learn to back up. You'll try turning left and right and making zigzags. Your instructors will take you on training runs in empty buses, to teach you the route and get you familiar with the daily challenges of the roadway. If you are hired to provide local transit, you'll have to memorize the routes. Some companies will offer a written test to prove you are capable of following directions and keeping to a schedule, because most routes are not a simple matter of getting from point A to point B and back again. In the beginning, you'll follow your route with an experienced driver. He or she will help you deal with questions and problems as they arise. He or she will also evaluate your performance and determine when you are ready to go out on your own.

School bus drivers have to pass a written test for the state. They have to show that they have the basic skills needed behind the wheel. There are usually one to four weeks of training in the classroom and on the pavement. You'll be taught about transit-related laws, policies, and regulations. Instructors will cover safe driving and emergency practices and driver-student relations, including ways to deal with discipline and student conduct.

How to Talk Like a Pro

Here are a few words you'll hear as a bus driver:

- ✦ **CDL** Drivers need a CDL (commercial driver's license) to drive any bus over 26,000 pounds or built to carry more than 16 passengers. For information on obtaining yours, contact your state motor vehicle department.
- ✦ **U.S. Department of Transportation** This U.S. department has rules and regulations related to driving buses, such as how many hours of service you can put in. Drivers cannot drive after working 60 hours in seven days or 70 hours in eight days, for instance.
- ✦ **School Bus Endorsement** To receive this endorsement, allowing you to drive students, you have to pass written and skills tests related to driving a school bus.

How to Find a Job

Among intercity bus drivers, the majority of openings will come from older workers leaving the field rather than from an overall increase, so competition will be stiff. Opportunities with local transit companies, however, are expected to grow faster than average because of expanding mass transit services in metropolitan areas, according to the Bureau of Labor Statistics. The number of positions for school bus driving will vary by state. Some states expect a decline in enrollment, while others, such as Arizona, are booming, so finding work will depend on where you live or are willing to go.

Positions are advertised in all the usual places: Web job boards, newspaper classifieds, state employment agencies. When you find an opening, your next job is to present yourself as the dependable employee they are hoping to hire. Read up on industry news online before your interview, show up on time, and fill out the employment form fully. Show your interest and understanding.

Secrets for Success

See the suggestions below and turn to the appendix for advice on résumés and interviews.

- Driving a bus is more about driving people around than it is about driving from place to place, so develop your customer service skills, your smile, and your sense of humor.
- Traffic and crowds are regular parts of the bus driver's work life; learn not to stress about things outside your control.

Reality Check

Senior drivers get the best routes, so as a junior driver, you may find yourself taking part-time, substitute, or "special" runs for a while, until you earn your spot.

Some Other Jobs to Think About

- Limo or taxi driver. If you're good at dealing with people and like to drive, the opportunity to drive individuals or small groups in a taxi or limo could work out well for you. Your daily route will not be fixed, as it often is as a bus driver; you will drive where your passengers need to go.

✦ Heavy equipment operator. If you are comfortable moving large machinery, your coordination might serve you well as an equipment operator, particularly of vehicles used in construction.

✦ Truck driver. Driving a truck can be like driving a bus, minus most of the hassles of dealing with people. If the road casts a spell on you more than people do, this may be the way to go.

How You Can Move Up

✦ Go into management. Drivers with management skills rise to the rank of supervisor. They take over personnel concerns and stay on top of industry issues.

✦ Become a dispatcher. If you're organized, you can be responsible for sending drivers on assigned routes and check on the schedules.

✦ Teach. There are drivers who become driving instructors. You can help bring up the next generation of drivers by teaching them everything you've come to know.

✦ Become a private owner and operator, if you're a driver with an entrepreneurial spirit.

Web Sites to Surf

United Motorcoach Association. This site includes industry news and general information on motor coach driving and related issues. http://www.uma.org

National School Transport Association. For similar news and information as it relates especially to driving school buses, check in on this site. You'll find a way to earn awards as well. http://www.yellowbuses.org

Be your own boss during your shift

Taxi Driver and Chauffeur

Use your driving skills to your advantage

Help people get where they need to be

Taxi Driver and Chauffeur

NASCAR is not the only venue for professional drivers. Taxi drivers and chauffeurs earn their livings behind the wheel too. Taxi drivers ferry passengers from place to place in urban settings, where residents do not necessarily have cars of their own and where tourists so often need transportation. In large cities, potential passengers flag down cars. The car company might also dispatch assignments that people have called in. Chauffeurs offer prearranged rides and are employed by individuals, agencies, and companies. Some chauffeurs specialize in transportation between airports and bus terminals and passenger destinations. Others also serve as executive assistants in the course of their work. The work of taxi drivers and chauffeurs is, indeed, all over the map!

Is This Job for You?

Would the job of taxi driver or chauffeur be a good fit for you? To find out, read the following questions and answer "Yes" or "No."

Yes	*No*	**1.**	Do you like working in an unstructured environment?
Yes	*No*	**2.**	Do you enjoy driving?
Yes	*No*	**3.**	Do you keep your cool in bad traffic?
Yes	*No*	**4.**	Can you stay alert in all kinds of weather and at all times of day?
Yes	*No*	**5.**	Do you enjoy talking with people?
Yes	*No*	**6.**	Do you like being helpful?
Yes	*No*	**7.**	Can you work with very little supervision?
Yes	*No*	**8.**	Do you know basic auto mechanics?
Yes	*No*	**9.**	Are you a good driver?
Yes	*No*	**10.**	Are you courteous and responsible?

If you answered "Yes" to most of the questions, you may have what it takes to become a professional driver. To find out more about this career, read on.

Let's Talk Money

Taxi drivers, some working part-time, had a median salary of $20,000 to $40,000 in 2007, according to Salary Wizard. Chauffeurs brought in $23,000 to $66,000. Senior chauffeurs, who have more responsibility, filled jobs in the higher range. The median hourly earning for full- and part-time taxi drivers and chauffeurs was $9.78 in 2006 (or $20,342 a year), according to the U.S. Bureau of Labor Statistics.

What You'll Do

A New York cab driver moved an elderly couple and their two cats from a Manhattan apartment to a retirement home in Sedona, New Mexico, in the spring of 2007. The couple did not drive, and they did not want to fly with their cats in the hold of a plane. The fare ended up in the thousands of dollars, and the trip lasted more than a week, there and back. Major news outlets picked up on the story, so the cab was followed by photographers and reporters.

It is highly unlikely that you would have a fare like that one, or at least, not very often, but the story illustrates how interesting work as a driver can be. On a regular day, a taxi driver reports to a garage. The driver fills the tank of his or her car or van and checks the vehicle's vitals, as it were—lights, tire pressure, and fluids—and fixes anything that is out of order. During the day, the driver stays in contact, by phone or radio, with the company dispatcher, who offers assignments that have been called in. Drivers transport passengers and collect fares, usually based on the distance covered and the time that was taken. Drivers also receive a good portion of income through tips from passengers. Often, the driver gives the passenger a receipt and records the time and fees in a log.

Chauffeurs also start the day by checking their vehicles. They might vacuum the carpets and wash the windows. They might add air to the tires. A chauffeur's job is centered on customer service, so details make a difference. As a private chauffeur, you might pick up your client's newspapers and favorite form of coffee beverage. Every job is different.

Who You'll Work For

✴ Limo companies
✴ Local, state, or federal governments
✴ Paratransit firms
✴ Private businesses
✴ Taxi companies
✴ Wealthy individuals
✴ Yourself

Where You'll Work

Most drivers work in large metropolitan areas, where the tourist industry is big and residents have access to public transportation, so that they do not need to buy their own cars. But you could be a professional driver in just about any part of the country. The regulations vary, but there are several forms your work might take as a taxi driver. You might lease a cab from an owner-operator. In that case, you will usually be responsible for the vehicle's upkeep. The tradeoff is that you will not have to make the initial investment in the car or van. You might rent a taxi from a fleet, shift by shift. The company would then deduct your rental from the money you make. You might lease a cab with an option to buy. Or you may own a cab outright, maintaining your own license, which is sometimes called a medallion.

A chauffeur may own a vehicle, or he or she may drive one provided by a boss. It may be a government vehicle. In any case, you'll spend your time working on the road, so you'll have to be knowledgeable about streets and points of interest. Your passengers will expect you to know where you are going—and how to get there fast.

Let's Talk Trends

This is a field that is typically in need of workers, especially in fast-growing metropolitan areas. Federal legislation that calls for increased services for people with disabilities is adding to the pressure to fill additional jobs, according to the Bureau of Labor Statistics.

Your Typical Day

Here are highlights of a regular day for a big-city driver.

✓ **Collect passengers.** You drive to a taxi stand at the railroad station, where commuters are coming in for the day's work. You collect your first fare.

✓ **Take a break.** After driving several people to their destinations, you pull over near a park and enjoy the lunch you packed. You take a breather before heading out again.

✓ **Put your records in order.** At day's end, you turn in your log, complete with vehicle identification number, your name, and a record of your fares, the date, and the times.

What You Can Do Now

✴ Get to know the area where you hope to drive. Memorize streets and points of interest.

✴ Keep your driving record clean.

✴ Take special driving and safety courses offered at your school.

✴ Network with people who can give you good references.

✴ Volunteer to chauffeur an elderly neighbor from time to time.

What Training You'll Need

The requirements vary by location. But for starters, you will need to have a driver's license in good standing. Companies often review your records before hiring you. They might look at medical, criminal, credit, and driving records before deciding to trust you with a vehicle. You will have to have held a license for a certain number of years. You should have a good driving record with no indication of reckless behavior. You cannot have a DUI conviction (for driving under the influence of alcohol or drugs) or a sex offense on your record. You must be 21 years old and able to speak English. Some places require an English proficiency test, usually for listening comprehension. Counties and cities determine what additional licenses are required for taxi or limo drivers, so check with your local government offices.

Many companies will require you to get a commercial driver's license (CDL). These classes can last 80 hours or more. If you are going to try to drive a paratransit vehicle, for people with special needs, you

The Inside Scoop: Q&A

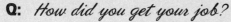

Joseph Rodriguez
Lead limo driver
Stamford, Connecticut

Q: *How did you get your job?*

A: I'm a Mexican chef by trade. I had my own restaurant in New Rochelle [New York]. A lot of my patrons were limousine drivers. I met them there and got to talking to them. When my restaurant folded because of construction on [a] bridge out front, I took up driving. It sounded good to me.

Q: *What do you like best about your job?*

A: The best thing I find with this company—I've worked for several companies over the years—is working in this company. The income is very good. Look, I'm well-dressed. I'm warm in the winter. I'm cool in the air-conditioning in the summer. And I meet so many nice people.

Q: *What's the most challenging part of your job?*

A: The most challenging part of the job is getting the jobs daily from my office and figuring out how to get from A to B. I'm old-school. I use maps. I know a lot of the people have GPS [Global Positioning System, which tells you locations using satellite signals]. But it's like working a puzzle every day. And I like it.

Q: *What are the keys to success as a limo driver?*

A: Be nice to people. Be professional with people. In my restaurant, I was a host. I learned how to talk with people. I brought all that over to driving. Believe me, it's all about [customer] service.

may need additional training so you know how to work the equipment and help your disabled or elderly passengers. You may have to learn how to operate a wheelchair lift, for example.

Certain companies have rules about appearance. You may have some kind of uniform and a cap. Or you may be required to wear a suit and tie. Your dress and bearing instill confidence in the passengers.

After landing the job, you may receive on-the-job training. You may have someone riding with you to make sure you fill out the logs correctly and know how to use the meters. There may be special safety training. After all, drivers often carry large amounts of cash. You need to know how to conduct yourself to keep your passengers, you, the vehicle, and the money safe and secure.

How to Talk Like a Pro

Here are a few words you'll hear about as a driver:

* **Driver abstract** This state record shows a driver's name, date of birth, mailing address, license class, endorsements, restrictions, current status of the license and its expected expiration, record of any suspensions or revocations of the license, accidents, and moving violations. Potential employers will check it.
* **Registration abstract** This has information about a particular vehicle, the name and address of the person who registered the vehicle, and the registration expiration date. As a driver, you want to make sure both abstracts are correct.
* **Owner-operator** If you buy your own cab or limo and maintain your own license (medallion), you are an owner-operator. You can then sublet the vehicle, if you like.

How to Find a Job

Drivers say that knowing someone is a key to getting a job. Joseph Rodriguez, featured in the interview section, arrived at his present cab company after being lured away from another one by other drivers. He has since helped his son find work there. Beyond networking, keep in mind that your money talks too. If you can swing the price of the vehicle and license, you can operate on your own and even sublet the car to others, to make more money during more hours. Just keep in mind, you will end up making more money because fewer people are taking a cut, but you will also have the full burden of maintenance. If you're not flush, you can rent or lease a vehicle, so the company that owns it takes money for the rental, and you keep the rest. Just find out what city ordinances say, and contact the department of motor vehicles in your state. Check Web job boards and employment agencies and classified ads for openings.

Secrets for Success

See the suggestions below and turn to the appendix for advice on résumés and interviews.

* Long-time drivers have noticed that pay increases with performance. In other words, when you drive with confidence and expertise, you will notice an increase in tips.
* Understand the social dimension of your role and allow yourself to become indispensable. Some drivers are executive assistants to the very wealthy. Such bosses are known to buy their drivers expensive cars and to pay very well to keep them.

Reality Check

Most cities have laws that require drivers to pick up fares—in all areas. Don't be ruled by stereotypes, but do have a safety plan.

Some Other Jobs to Think About

* Bus or other ground transit driver. If you like driving and meeting new people, you might want to consider driving a vanload or busload of passengers!
* Driver with sales route. Jobs are also available that involve driving goods, such as bakery items or office supplies, to retail outlets and acting as a sales agent for the company that employs you.
* Water transport. Similar positions are available on ferries, excursion boats, and other watercraft, if you enjoy time on the water.

How You Can Move Up

* Become an owner-operator. You can save up and buy your own ride.
* Run your own company. If you can attract investors, you can start your own fleet.
* Be a lead driver. By showing leadership skills, you can become the driver that your company places out front for other drivers to emulate at events, such as weddings or funerals.

Web Sites to Surf

National Limousine Association. Search this site to see how transportation workers unite to help one another with issues that are common to them all. http://www.limo.org

Taxicab, Limousine, and Paratransit Association. Here is a resource for drivers and an active network of professionals. http://www.tlpa.org

Get your career in flight

Airport Security, Baggage, or Maintenance Worker

Help keep travelers and shipments in the air

Join an active crew at a large or small airport

Airport Security, Baggage, or Maintenance Worker

Airports are like little cities, complete with neighborhoods and roadways and people in motion 24 hours a day. Airports are also major employers. From the patrols that guard the fields and runways to the screeners who check travelers' bags and luggage, jobs of all kinds abound at international and municipal airfields, and labor analysts predict that this will be the case through 2014, at least. With an increase in funding for the U.S. Department of Homeland Security, there has been a similar increase in security-related jobs. You can also find employment as a service provider, helping people with luggage and directing them to the right gate. Or you can work to maintain the grounds, from the parking lots to the hangars to the runways.

Is This Job for You?

Would a career working at an airport be a good fit for you? To find out, read each of the following questions and answer "Yes" or "No."

Yes	No	**1.**	Do you like to be around plenty of activity?
Yes	No	**2.**	Are you responsible and dependable?
Yes	No	**3.**	Do you have a good, clean record?
Yes	No	**4.**	Can you stay alert on your feet?
Yes	No	**5.**	Can you work well as part of a team?
Yes	No	**6.**	Can you take direction well?
Yes	No	**7.**	Would you enjoy an aviation-related career?
Yes	No	**8.**	Would you be able to handle working "on call?"
Yes	No	**9.**	Are you a problem solver who can foresee outcomes?
Yes	No	**10.**	Are you comfortable dealing with the public?

If you answered "Yes" to most of these questions, you might consider working in an airport. They are looking for good people!

What You'll Do

Security officers, also called access controllers, are needed to guard airfields and runways. Some are stationed near gates, while others patrol the grounds in vehicles. Yet others are in charge of guarding the perimeter of the area. Some carry weapons; others do not.

Let's Talk Money

According to Salary Wizard, security jobs paid $22,000 to $49,000 annually, as a median salary, in 2007. General maintenance earned a median salary of $23,000 to $42,000 yearly. The U.S. Bureau of Labor Statistics reported median annual earnings of $22,000 to $39,000 for this category of work in 2004.

You also find security personnel throughout the terminals. Screeners go through luggage and check passengers. They are trained to use X-ray equipment to detect weapons and other illegal items in carry-on baggage. As a screener, you do not have the power to arrest anyone, but you know to bring in airport police when necessary. It is your job to stay alert and communicate any problems related to passenger safety.

Many other workers are needed in airport maintenance. The physical plant of an airport needs to be in top operating order day and night, and crews are at work nonstop to provide that safe and accessible environment for the nation's airline passengers and the myriad of businesses that utilize airports. Lighting must be in working order. Electrical services must be maintained. The grass needs cutting. The shrubs must be managed. Snow and ice have to be removed from planes and runways. At any given time, you're likely to see someone painting walls or fixtures as you walk through a terminal. You'll find people repairing walls and seating and every other functional or decorative item.

There are 13,000 airports across the country, along with 4,000 heliports, and they all need staff. Just a fraction of airports concentrate on serving regular passenger airliners. The majority of airports serve individual pilots and their aircraft and are located throughout the country.

Who You'll Work For

✴ Aviation companies
✴ Department of Homeland Security
✴ Flight schools
✴ Hospitals or other heliports

Let's Talk Trends

Passenger travel dips with the economy, but long-term forecasts for the airline industry include a number of offsetting factors, cited by the Bureau of Labor Statistics: The population is aging. Disposable income is going up. International cargo traffic is increasing. Low-fare carriers are expanding. It all adds up to a 9 percent increase in related work though 2014.

✈ International or municipal airports
✈ Private airports and companies
✈ Security contractors
✈ U.S. military

Where You'll Work

As a member of airport security, you will work outside or inside, depending on the responsibilities of your job. Guards are posted in stations along roadsides. They may also roam the grounds by foot or in vehicles. You might work in a combination of environments throughout your career or even throughout the week.

As a screener, you'll spend your time indoors, within the terminals. Every airport is a warren of hallways and rooms between and surrounding cavernous spaces, where crowds roam between check-in desks and gates. You'll have a regular station at the point where paying passengers enter the gate area.

As a member of the airport maintenance crew, you could be working just about anywhere. You might maintain the runways. You might spend the majority of your time in the hangars. Or you might be part of the crew that cares for the other buildings, from the terminals to the towers.

You might be employed by a major messenger and package service and be surrounded by workers who are all employed by that same company. You might report to a large international airport. Or you might be in a smaller, municipal airport that mainly serves pilots who fly for pleasure, along with the pilots who work for local companies. This work takes many forms.

The Inside Scoop: Q&A

Jonathan Victor
Transportation security officer
LaGuardia International Airport, New York

Q: *How did you get the job?*

A: A few of my friends work for the TSA [Transportation Security Administration] and highly recommended this position, so I went online and applied.

Q: *What do you like best about your job?*

A: There are a lot of good things about this job. Personally, it makes me feel like I am making a difference in today's world by keeping people safe and secure before they travel. I am also a student, and the TSA is flexible where they offer different shifts to fit your schedule. Employees here are friendly and are willing to help and teach you, which makes you feel comfortable. The TSA also gives you an opportunity for advancement within the TSA or another federal agency.

Q: *What is the most challenging part of your job?*

A: The most challenging aspect is making sure no one gets through with a prohibited item or something that is dangerous to others.

Q: *What are keys to success to being an airport security worker?*

A: The keys to success are to be "on point" and alert. You must be aware of your surroundings, who and what is around you, in order to protect others.

Your Typical Day

Here are the highlights of a typical day for a screener.

✓ **Control the crowd.** The airport is busy all day long, but there are waves of crowds that are especially large. The crew keeps an eye out for lines that are backing up and opens more chutes as needed.

✔ **Help educate passengers.** An older woman has a bag of cosmetics, and a number of items are fluids not allowed on the plane. You explain, patiently and firmly, that the rules are the same for everyone, and you remove the items. A few kind words from you help ease her discomfort about the loss.

✔ **Take a break.** You've been stationed at the X-ray machine and need a break to stay alert. Your replacement steps in, and you go get some bottled water.

What You Can Do Now

✯ Security jobs require good communication skills, so work hard in your English and speech classes.

✯ Customer service is important in security, so take part-time or volunteer work that helps you develop those skills, such as in retail.

✯ To land a job in maintenance, try to find part-time or volunteer work that relates, such as building homes for Habitat for Humanity.

What Training You'll Need

Most training for these positions occurs on the job, under the eye of someone who has been in the position for a while—or someone in management. New hires often go through instructional classes, complete with videos that explain most aspects of airport management and how they tie together. These classes are typically about 12 hours total, because most of your training will occur on the job as you meet new and yet typical situations.

Since the terrorist attacks of September 11, 2001, the work of Homeland Security has taken on greater importance, and airport personnel are a big part of that picture. Airport security positions are among those that have experienced the most growth, as government agencies have identified areas within transportation that require tighter controls. Screeners are now called transportation security officers, to emphasize the importance of their tasks. These security officers undergo constant training to develop and broaden their awareness of threats. So as part of that staff, you can expect to be updated regularly on clues to human behavior that you should watch for and flag.

Airport maintenance crews value any skills that you can add to their departments, so any additional vocational of technical training you can add to your résumé will help you get a job. For instance, if you take training in heating and air-conditioning systems, your knowledge will be a plus in the hiring process. If you go to an airport or an aviation company with electrical skills and training, you are going to find your application put ahead of the rest. Technical and vocational schools offer many related classes, from grounds maintenance to plumbing. Even while in high school, you can be an apprentice to someone who does related work.

How to Talk Like a Pro

Here are a few words you'll bandy around in an air transportation career:

- ✦ **Department of Homeland Security** As the federal department that governs those who work to "anticipate, prevent, and react to anything from pandemics to hurricanes to terrorism," Homeland Security includes the Transportation Security Administration, which oversees airport security.
- ✦ **Transportation Security Administration** This federal administration protects transportation systems "to ensure freedom of movement for people and commerce." As a security screener, you work for them.
- ✦ **FAR** Federal Aviation Regulation is a common term for rules and regulations that cover aviation.

How to Find a Job

Security jobs require a conservative and professional appearance, so be sure you show up to your interview with conservative hairstyle, makeup (if applicable), and jewelry—and well-groomed nails. Have a list of contacts for any past employment and addresses and phone numbers for people who can serve as references. For this federal job with the Transportation Security Administration, you will have to pass a background or security check, so be aware that inquiries will be made, and any record of your past sayings or writings will be scrutinized. Do not tell your interviewer facts you only half remember. You could get yourself into trouble you don't deserve. And keep in mind that because of the security check, you will not be offered a job quickly. These things take time.

To work for airport maintenance, you usually need a driver's license and a good driving record; that way, you will be allowed to run the vehicles. Have proof of any mechanical certifications you have earned. And be sure to talk up any experience you have in related work.

If you research industry news, readily available on the Web, you can be first to know where new jobs will open. Job openings are posted in newspaper classifieds ads, on online job boards, and at employment agencies.

Secrets for Success

See the suggestions below and turn to the appendix for advice on résumés and interviews.

✶ Being dependable is the first order of business in all aspects of aviation. In many positions it also helps to be someone who can be called on at a moment's notice.

✶ For any airport security position, you will also need to be a stickler for rules and regulations.

✶ Be a problem solver, rather than a conflict creator.

Reality Check

Airlines operate at all times of the day or night. So you might have to do so too. Do not expect a 9-to-5 job.

Some Other Jobs to Think About

✶ Groundskeeper. Maintenance crews are needed for all kinds of businesses. You can specialize in outdoor or indoor work. Again, any mechanical training you earn will help you land a job.

✶ Hospitality workers. Baggage handlers are needed in the hotel and hospitality industry as well.

✶ Security guard. Not only airports need security staff to watch over the property and the people utilizing it. Many businesses, such as parking garages, hire people for these positions as well.

How You Can Move Up

✯ Advance into management. If you build your people skills, and volunteer for responsibilities, advancing is a real possibility.

✯ Learn computer skills. Take classes as needed to put yourself on the management track.

✯ Get advanced law-enforcement training.

Web Sites to Surf

Federal Aviation Administration. This national government agency oversees the aviation industry. On its site, you'll find information on applying for jobs and much more.   http://www.faa.gov

Transportation Security Administration. Here you will find information related to airport security and the many aspects of the work. http://www.tsa.gov

Move products and raw materials

Cargo Freight Agent or Dispatcher

Take pride in your contribution to the economy

See the big picture on distribution

Cargo Freight Agent or Dispatcher

Everything from turkeys to water tanks is produced or manufactured, packaged, and shipped with the help of cargo and freight agents. Every month of every year, agents and dispatchers line up schedules for loading and transport and take responsibility for their fulfillment. Whether the items travel by plane, train, ship, or truck— or some combination of methods—someone arranges for their pickup and delivery. Cargo transport is a vital, ongoing service, offering steady employment. For instance, rail and truck freight between the U.S. and Canada was worth $38.1 billion in February 2007. Between the U.S. and Mexico, it was worth $21.5 billion, according to the U.S. Bureau of Transportation Statistics. So if you're a detail-oriented person who likes getting things done, the shipping business is an active sector of the economy where you are needed.

Is This Job for You?

Would a career as a shipping and transportation agent send you in the right direction? To find out, read each of the following questions, and answer "Yes" or "No."

Yes No **1.** Are you a good listener who can keep track of conversation details?

Yes No **2.** Can you manage your time well and meet deadlines?

Yes No **3.** Can you analyze and solve practical problems?

Yes No **4.** Do you have the guts to make decisions, correcting them as needed?

Yes No **5.** Do you like coordinating events?

Yes No **6.** Can you communicate well in speech and writing?

Yes No **7.** Are you responsible and dependable?

Yes No **8.** Can you get people to cooperate?

Yes No **9.** Do you work well independently?

Yes No **10.** Can you happily deal with variables you cannot predict?

If you answered "Yes" to most of these questions, you may have what it takes to make a great cargo freight agent or dispatcher. To find out more about these careers, read on.

Let's Talk Money

These jobs have many titles, from freight broker to drop shipment clerk. But a general dispatcher earned $26,000 to $51,000 annually in 2007, depending on the number of years he or she had been working. That's according to Salary Wizard. The median hourly wage was $17.84, or $37,107, according to the 2006 data from the U.S. Bureau of Labor Statistics.

What You'll Do

Your title might be ship broker, documentation clerk, or any of a number of others, but the basic tasks and responsibilities are similar. You and the rest of your team will be in charge of keeping things moving! You might be responsible for transporting goods among departments within a company, or you might arrange freight deliveries for any number of clients and numerous destinations, if you work for a company that sells its shipping services to other businesses. In either case, you would use the most convenient and cost effective packaging and modes of transportation.

As a cargo or freight agent, you may be directly in charge of the packing of items, or in making sure others do the work. It's important to close containers tightly and make sure the goods will ship safely, within packing materials that do their job but are not wasteful. That may sound simple enough, but packing test tubes is one kind of challenge, and loading explosives is quite another.

Whether you are directly in charge of packing or not, the work is not a simple matter of packing things and sending them along. You keep track of the products and merchandise, using modern tracking methods, such as scanning bar codes. A big part of the job is taking care of documentation, noting how many items started off from point A and how many made it to point B. Sometimes that involves paying freight or postal fees. Other times, it means you have to find out why the numbers are off. You trace anything that was lost and figure out ways to keep that kind of thing from happening in the future.

Who You'll Work For

★ Air carriers

★ Distribution centers

★ Government agencies

★ Manufacturing companies

★ Marine carriers

★ Retail outlets

★ Train companies

★ Trucking companies

★ The U.S. Postal Service

Where You'll Work

These jobs are found in every corner of the country. The details of your work environment will depend on the kind of employer you have. Most agents work in an office environment, but many are also at docks for part of the day. If you were to take a job with a big retailer, such as a large furniture company, you might have a cubicle in a shared office where you keep your files and your computer. But you might also spend part of the day in the back of the store, where deliveries are made. There, small trucks, forklifts, and related equipment move containers from semitrucks to storage. If you work for a messenger and package service, you might have a small office in front of the ground transport station and spend your day going back and forth between the station and your desk. If you work for a distributor, such as a fruit and vegetable company, you might spend most of your time on the docks, checking on deliveries and keeping people motivated. You may have an office near an air freight terminal.

Let's Talk Trends

The job growth in this field is expected to be as fast as average, according to the Bureau of Labor Statistics. But within manufacturing, there is pressure to make distribution more efficient. This means strong job candidates will find plenty of opportunity within the field, say industry insiders.

Your Typical Day

Here are highlights of a typical day for a freight agent.

✓ **Clock in.** You check your "in" basket on your desk and in your computer for messages about deliveries made overnight. You get an updated picture of the work that will need to be accomplished during the day.

✓ **Make contacts.** You check in with people in other parts of the delivery system, such as the trucking dispatcher.

✓ **Take a load off!** You go to the dock and check boxes, keeping track with a scanner so not every little number has to be recorded by hand.

What You Can Do Now

✴ Take math and business classes in high school.

✴ Get part-time work that relates to the field. You might, for instance, work in a grocery store as a stocker and help with deliveries.

✴ Look for vocational training in logistics to help your résumé stand out.

What Training You'll Need

Much of what is most important in this work you will learn on the job, usually from another agent. Many companies have formal training programs, which could last from a day to several weeks depending on the special concerns of the industry you are in. So much of your energy should go into making contacts out in the field. But you can prepare for the field while you are in high school by taking related electives (for instance, business classes). You will need to communicate clearly and well, so pay attention in your English classes. You will be working with practical numbers all the time, so math will come in handy. Your skills on the phone will be very important, so practice, when you can, being clear and concise on the phone. You want to have a friendly but efficient manner for your on-the-job contacts. So develop a "business" phone voice.

Another big component of the work is customer service, so read up on books or attend seminars with this focus. Your counseling

The Inside Scoop: Q&A

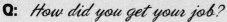

Ken Lewis
Freight agent
Clearwater, Florida

Q: *How did you get your job?*

A: I actually found [this company] online. It's Internet driven. I've been in sales all my life. The thing that's different about what we're doing here is there's lots of customer service.

Q: *What do you like best about your job?*

A: Number one is that if you do the right things, time just flies by. Personally, the way I look at it is that every day is a challenge. They're like snowflakes. No two are exactly the same.

Q: *What's the most challenging part of your job?*

A: Well, for us, and I'm not saying this is for all freight agents, [what's most challenging is] we are dealing with novice shippers. A lot of people think you're sending a little brown truck. Then they see this [big truck] pull up. And they also don't realize for the most part that freight has to be packed correctly. I had a guy shipping a 3,000-pound wrecking ball. I'm like, "How's it packaged?" And he's like, "It's a wrecking ball." But think about that ball rolling around in the back of a truck.

Q: *What are the keys to success to being a freight agent?*

A: We have about 25 agents here. Some are very successful. And some are not very successful. The key is the customer service work. Everybody can take your money. But when something goes wrong, if I don't take care of it, there's a problem.

office should be able to guide you to related programming. Within business, there are related apprenticeship programs you can find at the U.S. Department of Labor Career Voyages Web site at http://www.careervoyages.gov/apprenticeship-main.cfm. Any kind of experience in shipping operations is going to get you noticed, so look for part-time work that can serve as your first step in your shipping career. You might be able to get work at a local department store, for instance. If so, volunteer for any task related to the shipping department, especially work that gets you familiar with hand calculators. Learn early to respect the concerns of the shipping department; your practical knowledge will help you stand out among job candidates.

How to Talk Like a Pro

Here are a few words you'll hear as a freight agent:

- ✸ **Couriers** These are people who deliver letters, documents, and packages.
- ✸ **Dispatchers** This is the term for workers who distribute work loads among the people making deliveries.
- ✸ **Drop shipment** In this kind of delivery, the goods are left where the truck parks.

How to Find a Job

To find a job, be alert for job contacts among people you know and their families and friends. In shipping as in most lines of work, people in the know say having a contact is the most important variable in getting a job.

Jobs as freight agents are listed in newspaper classified ads, at employment agencies, and on Web job boards. Once you get an interview, be sure to bring up any related work you may have done and any additional related classes you took in or outside of high school. Fill out the application fully; being able to communicate in writing and taking care of details are important in this line of work, so you want to show a prospective employer, right from the start, that you "get it." Be on time, because timeliness is an important attribute. Everything about this job is about keeping to a schedule and respecting other people's time.

Secrets for Success

See the following suggestions and turn to the appendix for advice on résumés and interviews.

✦ On an online forum for freight agents, most pros advise novices that nothing beats on-the-job training; however, the agent identified as "John in Ohio" says, "A certificate of training from a brokerage school is not necessary, but it will add to your résumé."

✦ Every job is social, and many lead to further opportunities. You never know whom you can learn from.

Reality Check

You need to be highly organized to succeed in this field, so be honest with yourself: Can you keep all the balls in the air?

Some Other Jobs to Think About

✦ Office administrators. Your organizational skills and dependability are needed in private and government offices.

✦ Production, planning, and expediting clerks. Your skills with communication and numbers are needed in other aspects of manufacturing as well as beyond the shipping department.

✦ Weighers, measurers, checkers, and samplers. If you're organized and like to keep track of things, you might find satisfaction as someone who measures materials and equipment, using scales, hand calculators, and more.

How You Can Move Up

✦ Move into management. Taking additional business courses will help you.

✦ Consider an international job. As you gain experience and contacts, you might work for an international distributor, with travel opportunities. The crux of this line of work is the ability to make a decision and follow through. Sure, you will make an occasional mistake. But all you have to do is own up to it and learn from it.

✦ Do not hesitate to branch out. Direct your career in a way in which you learn to see the product and related services from as many perspectives as possible. The more multidimensional your understanding, the more you can manage your career.

Web Sites to Surf

Airforwarders Association. Read here for information on an association dedicated to the air freight business and all its concerns.
http://www.airforwarders.org

American Trucking Associations Inc. At this site, you can get an overview of the trucking business and its regulations.   http://www.truckline.com

Get your career on track

Train Track Maintenance Worker

Travel the rails, working for the railroad

Enjoy stable work in transportation

Train Track Maintenance Worker

For billions of tons of freight and for millions of passengers annually, rail is the way to go. For thousands of train track maintenance workers, keeping the overland, subway, and elevated tracks maintained and safe is the first order of business. Rail repair, which was once done by hand by large teams of workers called gandy dancers, is now handled by smaller crews with specialties like welding or switch maintenance. Maintenance workers run on-track vehicles and machinery, much of it heavy, to pull and insert spikes, extract and insert ties, tamp gravel, and much more. These jobs offer lasting benefits: Good health and retirement packages, days filled with fresh air, and the satisfaction of knowing you've helped keep passengers and cargo safe as you've detected and fixed flaws in the tracks.

Is This Job for You?

Would a career as a train track maintenance worker be a good fit for you? To find out, read the following questions and answer "Yes" or "No."

Yes	No	**1.**	Do you enjoy running big machinery?
Yes	No	**2.**	Do you have good strength and stamina?
Yes	No	**3.**	Are you responsible and dependable?
Yes	No	**4.**	Do you like solving problems?
Yes	No	**5.**	Can you work as part of a crew?
Yes	No	**6.**	Would you be comfortable working at nights sometimes?
Yes	No	**7.**	Do you like being outdoors?
Yes	No	**8.**	Do you appreciate the importance of the U.S. rail system?
Yes	No	**9.**	Can you follow safety procedures?
Yes	No	**10.**	Could you dedicate yourself to keeping tracks in optimal condition?

If you answered "Yes" to most of the questions, maybe you should be working on the railroad. To find out more about this job, read on.

Let's Talk Money

Railroad workers, across categories, earned $31,000 to $44,000 annually, according to 2007 data from Salary Wizard in 2006. Rail track maintenance workers earned a median hourly salary of $19.23, or $39,998 yearly, according to the U.S. Bureau of Labor Statistics.

What You'll Do

Maintenance work is often done from 7 p.m. to 4:30 a.m., when fewer trains need to rumble. But sometimes there is a need to work around the clock. Rail companies and railroad unions are mindful of making certain their maintenance workers—and others—get adequate rest, however. So don't expect to be called to do all the work yourself! You can expect, however, to be operating heavy equipment. You might be part of a tie gang, a surfacing gang, or a welding gang. These crews generally consist of two to seven people.

The ties alone weigh 200 pounds each, and 10 to 20 percent of them are being replaced at any given time. As time goes on, the weight of the trains compresses the ballast (coarse stone chips) under the tracks, and there is a need to resurface the area to lessen the bumps that passengers feel. Machines like tampers and regulators area called into action to lift track, compact the ballast below, and then straighten the track back in place. Workers in surfacing gangs sweep loose ballast back over the area that was just tamped before moving on to the next project. Other workers, in welding gangs, attempt to eliminate rail joints, to make the ride quieter inside the trains. Welders use air compressors, generators, power tools, heaters, welders, and grinders to get the job done. Other teams are charged with making inspections, often in a kind of pickup that can run on roads or rails. At times, they deal with spills.

You may use ultrasonic equipment to find flaws that can't be seen with the eye. You may be sent out in the weed-killing machine. With electronics training, you may repair signals or telecommunications equipment.

Let's Talk Trends

In 1980, the rail industry was deregulated. After that, there were shake-ups as companies merged and duplicate lines were eliminated. Now, fewer companies are running more trains than ever on fewer tracks, so the need for fast, reliable upkeep is greater than ever. And as Jeff Moller, executive director of operations for the Association of American Railroads said, "The jobs won't be shipped off to Asia."

Who You'll Work For

✴ Construction companies
✴ Interstate train systems
✴ Manufacturing companies
✴ Mining companies
✴ Municipal train systems
✴ Passenger lines
✴ Streetcar companies
✴ Subway systems
✴ Train track maintenance companies

Where You'll Work

Trains come in all sizes and are built for many purposes. Miniature trains take children in circles around zoological gardens. Giant engines cross the country, towing scores of trailers and delivering tons of goods. Railroads provide an important link across the states, carrying passengers, raw materials, and finished goods from place to place, so you could work just about anywhere.

Railroads comprise approximately 150,000 miles of maintained track nationwide. Trains run from the California seashore to the mountaintops; the busiest tracks are concentrated around Chicago and throughout the Northeast corridor. Amtrak passenger trains serve most major cities. That company is most active in the Northeast, running trains from Washington, D.C., to Boston and back again. In metropolitan areas, such as New York City, subways and light-rail systems transport passengers between homes and jobs.

The Inside Scoop: Q&A

Adam Ontiberos
Track foreman
Dodge City, Kansas

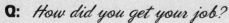

Q: *How did you get your job?*

A: I got it by word of mouth. I had experience in construction. To me, that's the same thing as working on the railroad. But anyway, I had to go through the training. Within four months, I was sent to FRA [Federal Railroad Administration] school [for a week-long class]. They needed a foreman here.

Q: *What do you like best about your job?*

A: To be honest with you, I like the pay and benefits. It has good job security. The railroad takes care of its people.

Q: *What's the most challenging part of your job?*

A: It's a challenge going out there and working with all this equipment, making sure the track is stable enough for these big locomotives going from the West Coast to the East Coast . . . . They've got these D cars [rail detector cars] that come across, checking the tracks [looking for moisture on the rails and determining which rails need replacing]. Generally they're going to find defects on your track. You might be told you've got seven or eight defects out there—and [you'll need to] go out and fix all seven or eight that day.

Q: *What are the keys to success to being a train track maintenance worker?*

A: I'd suggest that the wind of opportunity is here on the railroad. You can go as far as you want to; the sky's the limit. It's not what it's put out to be. It's a good job. If you're into traveling, it's the way to go. You just need the attitude and skills to get you there. If you want to be a track laborer and make a decent wage, or if you want to get a degree, your bachelor's, and work in the office, the railroad will help you get your education, as long as the work is railroad-related.

Subways and streetcars run over the surface, through underground tunnels, or even on elevated tracks, such as the famous El train in Chicago. Some tracks are in recessed settings within city streets.

Maintenance work is available wherever track has been laid, so you might find yourself working just about anywhere from sea to shining sea. The work is available internationally as well (though you will have be well-versed in the measuring systems and standards of any region where your skills may be applied). But one thing is certain. Most train maintenance workers are outside in all kinds of weather, keeping the trains going and the economy strong.

Your Typical Day

Here are the highlights of a typical shift as a train track maintenance worker.

- ✔ **Set up the job.** You have been charged with running the grinder. You work to prepare the rail surface before it is welded.
- ✔ **Do finishing touches as you go along.** After the new welds are made, you smooth them over before moving on.
- ✔ **Work through the night.** As day breaks, your team has completed as many welds as you had hoped to finish. But you'll be back after your day off tomorrow to do more.

What You Can Do Now

- ⚡ Look for related vocational training. Take shop and find paid or volunteer work related to the construction industry.
- ⚡ Take science classes like earth science so you understand forces of nature.
- ⚡ Read as much as you can about trains and tracks. Become familiar with the parts and terms.

What Training You'll Need

Much of what you need to know, you will learn on the job either through day-to-day interactions with other employees or in training classes arranged by your employer. To land that job, you'll want to show early interest in the field. In high school take technology classes, math classes, and sciences classes—and stay in shape. "You're going to be outside," says Al McNulty, manager of structures training at Johnson County Community College, in Kansas. "You need stamina and the aptitude of a mechanic or a construction worker. You need to be analytical and use math skills for measuring."

Most railroads have an engineering department that is broken into specialties: the track, signals, structures, telecommunications, welding, and work equipment departments. People are funneled into the departments that best match their developed skill sets, but they can move around as they become known quantities within. Track maintenance requires problem solving, measuring, and a basic knowledge of the practical sciences. For work in the signals or telecommunications department, knowledge of computers and electronics is needed. So take related classes in high school, or technical or community college if this interests you.

You will need to be a legal adult to be hired. It is also likely you will have to pass some kind of drug testing. The minimum education is a high school diploma, but you can stand out from the pack if you have taken vocational training or have related part-time or full-time work or volunteer experience. It is interesting to note that many workers who begin in the rail yard or doing maintenance later are given the opportunity to train as engineers or conductors if they so choose. Keep in mind, as well, that most railroad workers are part of a union. Others are considered exempt employees. In either case, there are opportunities to continue your education while on the job, as long as your field of study relates to the work you are doing.

How to Talk Like a Pro

Here are a few words you'll hear and use as a track maintenance worker:

- ✴ **Hi-rail (or Hyrail)** These vehicles are used to perform visual inspections of the tracks. They are specially equipped pickup trucks that can go from rails to roads, using rubber or steel tires, as needed.
- ✴ **Tamper** A tamper is a self-propelled vehicle that can lift track. It has vibrating heads that can penetrate and compact the ballast. It is called into action to resurface tracks.
- ✴ **Class of track** The class of track determines the speed limits and whether the track can take passenger trains. The lowest class is called "excepted track." Only freight trains can run there—at 10 m.p.h. Class 9, the highest, limits trains to 200 m.p.h.

How to Find a Job

Adam Ontiberos (see "The Inside Scoop") landed his job because he had knowledge of the construction industry, and the local railroad office was looking for people with his skills. As in other industries, knowing people is always a plus. "It's nice if someone recommends you for an interview," says McNulty, a veteran of the Burlington Northern Santa Fe. So seek out contacts with present railroad employees.

You can find work through human resources departments on site at railroads and rail transit systems and through job boards in newspapers and on the Internet. Your state employment service office will have full listings. Opportunities among long-distance crews, says the Bureau of Labor Statistics, are expected to be better than those for yard jobs. But people in the field say there are plenty of yard workers in their 50s who expect to retire (with benefits) at age 60. Though the jobs of running trains and repairing track are becoming increasingly technical and mechanized, and repair crews no longer have to be as large as they once were, this doesn't change that more trains are running on fewer tracks, so immediate repair is a pressing issue.

Secrets for Success

See the suggestions below and turn to the appendix for advice on résumés and interviews.

✶ On this job, you'll need to make fast decisions about repairs and get them done right the first time. As one rail executive put it, "We don't have time to get people out there all the live-long day."

✶ Be reliable and establish yourself as a people person. The ability to get along with and establish communications among all kinds of people is needed to move forward.

Reality Check

If the idea of being outdoors sounds good to you, but you haven't really lived that way, strive to get yourself out in the elements before committing to this line of work. It's healthful, but this is no desk job.

Some Other Jobs to Think About

⭐ Building maintenance. If you have the know-how to repair track, you could apply your skills to office and apartment buildings instead.

⭐ Rail yard engineers. In this position, the engineer operates engineers within a rail yard. Some places employ dinkey operators, who drive small engines within plants, mines, quarries, and construction spots. Hostlers drive engines without attached cars within the yard.

⭐ Yardmaster. Yardmasters act as coordinators of the workers in railroad operations and traffic. They run switches that divert trains onto tracks where they will be coupled or uncoupled. They tell engineers where to run.

How You Can Move Up

⭐ Learn all you can. In the railroad, your in-depth knowledge of operations can prepare you for management.

⭐ Take advantage of training opportunities. You never know where a session may lead you.

⭐ Sign up for related classes, such as railroad health and safety and rail maintenance, in community or technical colleges or at a university. Many railroad companies offer education benefits.

Web Sites to Surf

Association of American Railroads. This site has information on everything having to do with railroads. http://www.aar.org

American Railway Engineering and Maintenance of Way Association. This group celebrates on the design and construction of railways and the maintenance of way with awards and more. http://www.arema.org

Take control of a truck and your future

Refuse Worker or Hauler

Enjoy the benefits of stable, service-oriented employment

Join the fast-growing field of waste management

Refuse Worker or Hauler

It used to be that no one thought to classify refuse, or garbage, into grades of plastic, glass, newspaper, or yard waste—or even to think about it much. But with the "greening" of America, people have learned to recycle materials, and waste management has become a science. The refuse crew is an important part of recycling—trash collectors and recyclers are on the front lines in waste management. These days, there are nearly 150,000 positions for refuse and recycling collectors, according to the U.S. Bureau of Labor Statistics, with many more jobs in other aspects of material movement. Many of the jobs require strength and dependability, especially for those workers who lift and empty bins and cans. Other workers learn to operate large machinery, such as the hydraulic lift truck that takes the dumpsters skyward.

Is This Job for You?

Would working as a refuse worker or hauler be a good fit for you? To find out, read the following questions and answer "Yes" or "No."

Yes   No   **1.** Do you like helping people in their daily lives?

Yes   No   **2.** Are you physically fit?

Yes   No   **3.** Are you disciplined when facing repetitive tasks?

Yes   No   **4.** Are you a good driver?

Yes   No   **5.** Are you good at taking and giving directions?

Yes   No   **6.** Can you be patient with customers?

Yes   No   **7.** Does working early in the morning sound good?

Yes   No   **8.** Do you like being outdoors?

Yes   No   **9.** Can you find meaning in work that other people might shun?

Yes   No   **10.** Can you tolerate smells and dirt and know how to keep above it?

If you answered "Yes" to most of the questions, you might consider a career in waste management. To find out more about this job, read on.

Let's Talk Money

You will earn $20,000 to $34,000 as a median salary at the start, according to 2007 Salary Wizard figures. According to the U.S. Bureau of Labor Statistics, collectors made $13.93 as a median hourly salary in 2006 (or $28,974 per year), with first-line supervisors earning more than a median hourly wage of $19 (or $39,520 per year).

What You'll Do

Among refuse workers, there is a division between those who perform most of the labor and those who operate the vehicles and machinery that move the material. But they all work as part of a team to transport tons of refuse from homes and businesses to recycling centers, dumps, and landfills. The group holds power in whatever municipality it operates in; nothing slows down a city faster than a strike of refuse workers.

As you can imagine, the work takes stamina. If you are thinking about this job, you have to ask yourself how much weight you can lift. And you have to be someone who is smart about his or her movements. You'll have to stoop and crouch, and you'll have to lift heavy cans and objects.

The particulars of the job vary by location. Local governments have differing requirements for the classification of recyclables, lawn and other green waste, and large-item or construction pickups. The waste management companies that contract for the work have their own requirements as well. However it works out in your location, you will find that the weeks have patterns. One day there will be one route, perhaps for general waste. Another day you might be assigned to another town. Your challenge will be to complete the work quickly, cleanly, and efficiently.

One of the main issues of the job is personal safety for the work crew. It is not uncommon for drivers of other vehicles to misjudge the size of garbage trucks. In the early morning confusion, it is up to the refuse workers to watch out for themselves and for one another.

Who You'll Work For

★ Waste management companies
★ City governments

✴ Federal government
✴ U.S. military
✴ Private recyclers
✴ Rural townships
✴ State governments
✴ Temporary work agencies

Where You'll Work

Generally, you will start your day at a garage. You will probably be responsible for maintaining the vehicle you run, so you will spend some time filling the gas tank and checking fluid levels and tire pressure. You may even wash the truck, as needed. You will travel between the refuse center or landfill and your route. So a good part of the time, you will be on the road.

Usually, you will work outside, though you will also spend time indoors, in the shelter or semi-shelter of the refuse station, if you help sort collections. The collections will be dirty, and there is no getting around that, but you will be trained to dispose of the items safely, in a manner that protects your health.

Your place of employment could be anywhere in the country. Throughout the United States, refuse workers generally work on a one-person or two-person packer, driving the collection truck along an assigned route and working as a team to get the collections done. In cities, you might be following a pattern of alleys and streets. In suburbs, you would most often be following stops at driveways. You will be emptying trashcans of all sizes and collecting recyclables, such as newspapers, from special containers. Your office will be the cab of the truck. There, you will keep track of special notices, which must be left for customers who are not complying with the rules, and prepare your daily reports, a log of anything odd that happens or does not happen along your route.

Let's Talk Trends

The amount of refuse people generate is only getting larger. Material movers held more than 5 million jobs, according to the recent figures. These jobs are here to stay.

Your Typical Day

Here are some features of a typical day as a refuse worker or hauler.

✔ **Start your route.** You go from one pickup point to another, getting your exercise as you complete the job.

✔ **Help your customer.** Along your route, you find that someone new has moved into a house. The family is not placing the recyclables in the correct bins. You take the time to ring the doorbell and leave a note with instructions.

✔ **Move to a special assignment.** A couple of crews have been pulled in to work on graffiti removal downtown. You meet at the end of the day to discuss how you will tackle the job.

What You Can Do Now

✯ Plan to get commercial driver's license; you will need one. Information is available from your state motor vehicle department.

✯ Look for part-time work or volunteer experience operating a truck. Employers will often look for this experience. So if you can gain it, for instance, by working for a small company, do so.

✯ Get and stay in shape. You need plenty of strength to do this work in a time-efficient manner.

✯ Read up on what materials can and can't be put out with regular refuse and what materials are acceptable for recycling.

What Training You Will Need

Contact your state to find out which steps you need to take to earn a commercial driver's license. Then follow through with the program officials require. You will need a clean driving record and will probably be required to undergo a medical examination. Refuse workers need to be in good health; there is plenty of heavy lifting involved, quite literally.

Most of your work-related training will come from the private company or government agency that hires you. You will be taught about routes and procedures, which are especially important in special pickups. You will probably be taught some basics about customer service, because dealing with customer complaints and

The Inside Scoop: Q&A

Cleotha Williams Jr.
Driver
Las Vegas, Nevada

Q: *How did you get your job?*

A: My father had been a garbage truck driver for 19 years, and when I turned 17, I decided to follow in my father's footsteps and become one as well. Watching my father as I grew up, I knew that driving a garbage truck was a good steady job that helped him take care of his family. My father retired as a driver after 30 years of service.

Q: *What do you like best about your job?*

A: Waste disposal is a very important service that we provide to the community. I respect the importance of that role and the opportunity that I have to serve the community. As the driver of a garbage truck, you are the face of the company to the public. Each day I have an opportunity to meet customers and try to provide the best customer service I can. Also as a driver, I am able to work on my own. We have supervisors that we interact with, but most of the day we are on our own. It is important for us to be responsible and self-motivated.

Q: *What is the most challenging part of your job?*

A: Weather, of course, is one of the biggest challenges we face. Even if it is raining or snowing, the garbage still needs to be picked up. And the high temperatures of the summer can be especially draining. Physically, the job is challenging. Pushing large containers and lifting full cans over and over can be demanding. Our biggest challenge however, is safety. Most people do not realize how dangerous of a job this can be. You must always be completely aware of your surroundings, not just for your own safety, but the public's safety as well.

(Continued on next page)

(continued from previous page)

Q: *What are the keys to success to being a refuse hauler?*

A: The key for doing the best job you can is having the right mind-set. It is important to take pride in the job you do and challenge yourself to do the best job you can and exceed your customers' expectations.

questions is part of the job. You become, in effect, a company or government representative.

You should be given training to identify hazardous materials. So often people will place items in the trash that become a safety issue, mainly because of their lack of knowledge on the subject. There should be plenty of discussion of safe work practices, such as how to park the truck and deal with traffic flow. There will be training for the operation of the vehicles as well.

In the end, you need to know how to work independently with a minimum of instruction. You must be able to communicate clearly. You should be a punctual team player who can maintain congenial relationships with coworkers and customers. And you should operate every waking moment with safety foremost in your mind. It is likely that training sessions will continue to be offered to you, no matter where you are employed. Rules and regulations are updated constantly, so you should expect the same for your training.

How to Talk Like a Pro

Here are a few terms you may hear as a refuse worker or hauler:

✴ **OSHA** The letters stand for "Occupational Safety and Health Administration," which is part of the U.S. Department of Labor. Safety and training requirements for your job and others originate with it.

✴ **Waste management** That term encompasses the removal and storage of all levels of refuse and waste. It is a combination of business and science.

✴ **EPA** The letters stand for *Environmental Protection Agency.* Given the importance of proper waste management for a greener world, much of the work of a refuse crew falls under the EPA umbrella.

How to Find a Job

A little experience goes a long way, as does a contact within the industry. As with most job searches, your quest for work in refuse should take you to the newspaper's print or online classifieds, where many jobs are advertised, to Web job boards, and to your state employment agency. You can also find success by directly contacting waste disposal businesses in your area.

The person who interviews you is looking for someone dependable who can handle the customer relations issues that arise. So show up for your interview on time. Be sure to have all the information you will probably be asked for: Addresses and phone numbers for past employers, addresses and phone numbers for personal references, and proof of your commercial driver's license. Your days will typically begin early, and there is a chance you will be asked to work on weekends as well. Be prepared to say "yes" to any shift that is offered you. You can't earn seniority without getting the job first!

Secrets for Success

See the suggestions below and turn to the appendix for advice on résumés and interviews.

- In this line of work, being coordinated and flexible is important. One wrong bend and trash could scatter or your back could go out.
- Client contacts can be a significant part of your work, and sometimes you are the first person from the company that a frustrated client can talk to. Stand on the quality of your work and keep a pleasant outlook.

Reality Check

This job offers steady employment, solid pay, and a built-in exercise program—for practical people who like to know they have accomplished something each day. However, this line of work lacks prestige.

Some Other Jobs to Think About

- Crane and tower operator. In this line of work, you work mechanical boom and cable equipment, lifting and moving heavy objects and materials. These skills are especially needed in industrial and construction projects.

✯ Hand packer and packager. Your strength and organizational skills are needed to pack and package materials for shipment at loading docks in a variety of industries.

✯ Industrial truck and tractor operator. If operating the vehicle attracts you the most, consider a specialty as a large vehicle operator.

How You Can Move Up

✯ Learn the business from the ground up. In waste management, many supervisors and managers started this way, and so can you.

✯ Look for ways to improve the routes and work processes.

✯ Take classes at a technical or vocational college to prepare you for the scheduling and paperwork that will be required of you as a supervisor. Take communications classes as well.

✯ Earn awards for your good work.

Web Sites to Surf

National Solid Wastes Management Association. At this site, you'll find plenty of information on related safety and legal issues, along with industry news. http://www.nswma.org

Environmental Industry Association. This is the gateway for businesses related to the environment and waste. It features programs and events, including awards for refuse drivers. http://www.envasns.org

Sail into a fulfilled future

Water Transportation Worker

Let your love of the water land you a job

Train to work in shipping

Water Transportation Worker

Being part of a ship's crew is work that can satisfy both the adventurous and practical sides of you. Water transportation workers are needed to run commercial and private ships of all sizes. There were 72,000 official positions in the 2004 survey for the U.S. Bureau of Labor Statistics, yet the total number of seamen who did some kind of related work was probably twice that. With a mariner's license, issued by the U.S. Coast Guard, you can help provide passenger and cargo transport on local or international waters. You could be hired for an excursion vessel, a tugboat, a ferry, a deep-sea craft—the opportunities take many forms. Crews perform basic operational tasks, from steering the vessel to performing maintenance. You might serve on lookout, serve food, measure water depth, or operate pumps. Long-distance jobs generally hire out on a voyage-by-voyage basis, so adventure can be part of the job description.

Is This Job for You?

Would working as a merchant mariner be a good fit for you? To find out, read each of the following questions, and answer "Yes" or "No."

Yes   No   **1.** Do you enjoy working as part of a team?

Yes   No   **2.** Do you like traveling by water and the idea of working on a boat?

Yes   No   **3.** Are you comfortable not knowing what your next assignment will be?

Yes   No   **4.** Do you have good stamina to meet the demands of physical labor?

Yes   No   **5.** Do you respect the power of nature, such as storms and wind?

Yes   No   **6.** Do you take direction well?

Yes   No   **7.** Are you dependable yet flexible?

Yes   No   **8.** Do you have a basic understanding of mechanics?

Yes   No   **9.** Can you be away from home for days and even months?

Yes   No   **10.** Do you like being outside in all kinds of weather?

If you answered "Yes" to most of these questions, you may have the know-how to pursue a career on the water. To find out more about these jobs, read on.

Let's Talk Money

According to the U.S. Bureau of Labor Statistics data from 2006, water transportation workers earned an hourly salary of just over $19 in 2006. That's a mean, not an average. The mean annual salary was nearly $48,000. Beginners often earn minimum wage. Merchant mariners on oceangoing ships tend to earn higher wages than those who work on inland waterways, though international sailors often must wait between assignments.

What You'll Do

The term "merchant mariner" refers to a water transportation worker who is employed on a commercial ship—anything from a dredge to a cruise ship. You could be moving cargo or you could be taking passengers to jobs or on pleasure cruises, such as fishing expeditions. Just as there are any number of reasons why people might be on the roads, there are all kinds of quests that lead people out on the water and any number of employers who staff the vessels.

You might work as an assistant to the ship's engineer, maintaining and operating the pumps, boilers, generators, and engines. If so, much of your day might be spent below deck, if the ship is large. As a sailor, you maintain areas outside the engine and run the vessel. Sailors keep track of the waters and the weather and make sure the ship is in working order (outside the duties that engineers and their assistants perform). If you're on a ship on the ocean, the sailors with deeper understanding of the work are called able seamen or able-bodied seamen. If you work on a vessel that cruises inland waterways, the sailors are called deckhands. But much of the work they do is the same.

The crews you work with might be large or small, depending on your duties and where you sail. The larger the crew, the more spots for unlicensed seamen, such as cooks or oilers, who read temperature gauges and help with the machinery. In this line of work, you can decide how often you will go out to sea. Some mariners have other jobs on land and do a variety of things to keep money flowing.

Let's Talk Trends

The maritime shipping industry is contracting in the United States. But the government has recognized that having more ships flying U.S. flags is important to national security, so some cargo lines are getting government subsidies and are growing. There is growth in the cruise ship industry as well—especially around Hawaii.

Who You'll Work For

- ✻ Excursion or tourist firms
- ✻ International or national shipping companies
- ✻ Local patrols
- ✻ Marine educational facilities
- ✻ Private owners
- ✻ State or local governments
- ✻ U.S. military
- ✻ Water maintenance services

Where You'll Work

You might work anywhere there's water that's not frozen. You could be employed on rivers like the Mississippi or the Colorado, taking raw materials and finished products—or even steamship passengers—to their destinations. You might work in the Great Lakes region or on any number of bodies of water within the United States, hauling goods to manufacturers and to retail distribution centers. You might find yourself employed on a canal or stationed in a harbor. Or you might be out on the ocean, crossing into international waters.

If you are employed at a harbor or on one of the many rivers in the continental United States, you might have a regular eight-hour shift, or one that is slightly longer. You might be part of a regular crew on a small vessel that has regular runs. If you work on the seas, you might have active and inactive months, and each haul might vary quite a bit. But you'll spend your working hours on the part of the ship to which you have been assigned and your off hours in the living quarters.

The Inside Scoop: Q&A

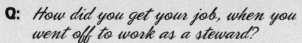

Caroline Ghiloni
Former ship's steward
Piney Point, Maryland

Q: *How did you get your job, when you went off to work as a steward?*

A: I lived in the area, and I was working for the military. But I had worked here [at the school] previously and had always wanted to sail aboard ship. Basically, I got my job through contacts.

Q: *What did you like best about your job?*

A: The work is very interesting. You have foreign travel. You have coastwise travel. The hours were early morning hours, and then you'd have time ashore. The money was very interesting too. Even though it takes you from your home sometimes for three, four months at a time, it's wonderful work. You would meet some interesting people, that's for sure.

Q: *What are the major challenges of the work?*

A: The major challenge if you work in a steward department is to make the food interesting. If you work in the deck department, you have to be ready to tie up; you have to be ready for anything. Able-bodied seamen working on deck have a lot of challenges; you're also on the bridge. Able bodies actually run the ship. The only time they call the captain is when they're coming into port or things like that.

Q: *What are keys for success on the seas?*

A: It's going out there and taking what training you've had and making something of it. It's also going back to school and getting more training. It's always a learning process. We hit some rough seas out there. But it's worth it. I miss it every day. It's something that gets in your blood.

Contrary to so many old movies about the sailing life, many modern ships have living quarters that are air-conditioned and soundproofed. Just don't expect private quarters; everything is usually shared. Sailors take advantage of advanced communications equipment to stay in touch with the folks back home.

Your Typical Day

Here are highlights of a typical day on the water.

✔ **Get to work.** The morning flies by; you are busy fixing the paint on the rails. You chip paint and then cover over those areas with white paint.

✔ **Break for lunch.** You meet with other crew members in the galley. The cook has prepared a special Southwestern meal, to honor the guy from Arizona who is having a birthday this week.

✔ **Move to another deck.** You are asked to help clean the top deck. The sun is brutal, but you do your work quickly and efficiently.

What You Can Do Now

✯ Look into the variety of licenses offered by the Coast Guard, and plan to earn what you need.

✯ Look into union training available for deckhands. To become an officer, you will need to look into earning a bachelor's degree at a maritime academy.

✯ Look for an apprenticeship with a pilot's association or towing company, which will enable you to do certain kinds of work. In fact, there are maritime high schools you can attend, such as Chapman School of Seamanship in Stuart, Florida.

What Training You'll Need

To operate a vessel or be an officer of a commercial vessel, you must work for and receive a Coast Guard license. These licenses vary in scope and the time needed to earn them. The details relate to the types of vessels you hope to operate and the kind of work you hope to do. This training is had through the U.S. Merchant Marine Academy and a few other maritime academies, which you can find listed online.

You'll end up with a written exam, a physical, and a drug screening. If you pass, you might receive a degree, a license, or even a commission. If you are unlicensed, you need to get a special document from the Coast Guard to work in deep waters, such as the Great Lakes or the oceans. What's more, there are special certifications required for sailors who haul liquid cargo. After all, operating a ship is much more complicated than driving a ground vehicle. The vessel's position must be monitored (you're not on a marked road). Hazards must be avoided. Engines must be maintained en route. Passengers and cargo must be accounted for; the ship's movements must be recorded. There is basic upkeep to attend to; someone must steer. You even have to keep track of how you've controlled pollution.

You need a working knowledge of water depth, currents, tides, and winds. And you need an entire crew, with everyone doing an integral part of the work at hand. To learn the job you hope to master, and to come to a basic understanding of the others, you need time on the water, under the tutelage of people who are already masters at what they do.

You can get formal training at a maritime school. You can get training at a school operated by a union. Or you can work your way from the bottom by taking a lower level job as an ordinary seaman and learning as you go.

How to Talk Like a Pro

Here are a few words or terms you should get used to tossing around:

- ✦ **Ordinary seaman** This crew member takes care of the most basic assignments, such as keeping watch or cleaning, painting, and maintaining the ship.
- ✦ **First, second, and third mate** Mates are deck officers. In ships that operate with more than one, they have numbers. The first mate is the chief deckhand.
- ✦ **Able-bodied seaman** This crew member can do the jobs of an ordinary seaman but will also take care of more specialized tasks, such as operating a forklift or guiding a helicopter to the flight deck.

How to Find a Job

Start with the Coast Guard, where you must apply to get a license or at least special papers to do most kinds of work on the water. For different jobs, you'll take different steps. But you will need some experience on the water and in some instances, training at institutes where you are likely to make the contacts you need to land a job.

About a quarter of merchant mariners belong to unions, such as Seafarers International Union, so it can make sense to follow union news and to network at related functions, as possible. Unions have hiring halls at major seaports. There, they organize and provide jobs for beginners and veterans.

You'll also find open jobs posted at employment agencies and on Web job boards. Many jobs will go first to people who hear by word of mouth. So keep lines of communication open with any and everyone you know who works in water transportation. Bear in mind that it doesn't always pay to be highly specialized in your skills; versatility matters more. So be a student of everything that has to do with ships.

Secrets for Success

See the suggestions below and turn to the appendix for advice on résumés and interviews.

- ✴ A former sailor who went on to own a shipping company has two hints for beginners. Number one, you need a "cast iron stomach." Number two, if you work on deck, leave your jewelry at home. "I almost lost a finger when I wore a wedding band," he says.
- ✴ Learn all duties. Become a master of all aspects of the ship. Do not be content to stick to one job the entire time.

Reality Check

This career can be hard on families because you can be away a lot. It depends on how you structure your time and which jobs you accept at which times of life.

Some Other Jobs to Think About

- ✴ Fisher. You can put your love of the water to work as a fisher who brings in catches while operating a vessel.
- ✴ Dock hand. There are jobs on docks in which people perform all kinds of services, from helping tourists aboard tour boats to renting canoes for fishing excursions.

★ Coast guard or navy. The military offers various ways to learn and earn a sea career while serving the country.

How You Can Move Up

★ Take classes. There is no reason you cannot earn a bachelor's degree in this field. It can translate to better assignments and pay.
★ Work your way up. Take your job seriously and prove your worth by being smart and dependable.
★ Join related unions and associations, and network. Take advantage of conferences and classes.

Web Sites to Surf

United Seamen's Service. This group is united to promote the welfare of U.S. seamen. http://www.uss-ammla.com

U.S. Coast Guard. Start here to read more about jobs and important maritime issues. http://www.uscg.mil

Run machinery that keeps the economy going

Manufacturing Equipment Operator

Know how building and manufacturing gets done

Build a sturdy career using your equipment skills

Manufacturing Equipment Operator

Operators run motorized machines, from presses to snowplows, using stationary equipment and moving vehicles. They support businesses and services from sawmills to satellites. You might hone hand-eye skills to work as a fabricator. Or you might use your coordination and "cool" to run heavy equipment, such as cranes or backhoes. These jobs might sound straightforward, but equipment is often highly computerized, so the skills can be quite specialized. And this is big business: In just one issue of the magazine for the International Union of Operating Engineers, featured construction projects included an $850 million stadium for the Indianapolis Colts and new wastewater treatment plants funded by a $15 billion congressional bill. Some operators go on to supervise projects; all perform duties integral to the smooth operation of the economy.

Is This Job for You?

Would working as an equipment operator work well for you? To find out, read each of the following questions, and answer "Yes" or "No."

Yes	No	**1.**	Do you have steady hands?
Yes	No	**2.**	Are comfortable with physical labor?
Yes	No	**3.**	Do you enjoy working as part of a team?
Yes	No	**4.**	Can you figure out mechanical processes on your own, but still take direction?
Yes	No	**5.**	Are you patient during long-term projects and able to work in chunks of time?
Yes	No	**6.**	Are you safety-minded around equipment?
Yes	No	**7.**	Do you enjoy operating and being around machinery?
Yes	No	**8.**	Do you "get" the mechanics of most machines?
Yes	No	**9.**	Are you fit and able to lift heavy objects?
Yes	No	**10.**	Can you recognize threats to safety and respond quickly?

If you answered "Yes" to most of these questions, you might consider making a career as an equipment operator. To find out more about this job, read on.

Let's Talk Money

As you can imagine, with so much variety in the work, the pay scale varies too. Much of the variation also depends on where you live. In 2007, heavy equipment operators were earning $33,000 to $55,000 as an annual median salary, according to Salary Wizard. In 2004 hourly wages, equipment operators of all stripes earned anywhere from $12 to $30, according to the U.S. Bureau of Labor Statistics.

What You'll Do

The core of the work calls for a safe and steady approach to the machinery in your care. Your job might require that you know how to operate any number of machines over the course of a project, or you might be expected to run just one, such as a concrete mixer, and keep it maintained and repaired. Part of the day might involve general labor functions, such as loading and unloading boxes of raw materials, or arranging stock. Another part of your schedule might involve paperwork, such as assigning control numbers to items before they are transported. It all depends on the industry and the size of the staff. In general, the smaller the operation, the more you will be called on to fill multiple functions. Yet the crux of your work will be your skill at the equipment operation, judging qualities like load weight and rotation distance and motor heat, balancing your workload, and keeping things running smoothly.

In many kinds of equipment operation, and especially when you are newest to the staff, you might be required to work irregular hours or in rotating shifts. In a 24-hour economy, you might be given the night shift. So be ready for these possibilities. Just remember that people who work nights say the shift has benefits, such as getting your errands done when fewer people are concerning themselves with day-to-day chores like grocery shopping. In many of the jobs involving heavy equipment, you will work outside. You will face all kinds of weather conditions, from the beautiful, sunny weather that might make you wish you were otherwise engaged to storm conditions that challenge your courage.

Who You'll Work For

✯ Construction companies

✯ Education and public welfare centers

✯ Home services and repair concerns

✯ Major manufacturers

✯ Municipalities—villages, towns, and cities

✯ Small manufacturers

✯ State and federal agencies

✯ Transportation firms

Where You'll Work

Of all the work described within this volume, the operation of light and heavy equipment is most varied. You might be running a boom mic for a local cable TV station. You might be operating a sweeper to clear roads. Or you could be helping to build skyscrapers by operating a crane that lifts other equipment. The variety of jobs that fall under this umbrella is virtually endless. Equipment operation is a key to building and manufacturing, so it is an important part of what keeps the economy functional.

When you operate smaller equipment, such as lathes, you are more likely to be working inside, in an environment controlled for safety. The larger the equipment, the more likely you are outside working on a big project, such as moving earth to build a subdivision. But there are exceptions to every rule.

Your shift might cover any time of the day or night, depending on the industry. Auto plants are lit all day and night, with different shifts arriving throughout the day. Small fabricators close their doors at dinnertime.

Let's Talk Trends

The amount of production and construction going on is tied to the economy and its ups and downs, but industry watchers say prospects through 2014 should be good for equipment operators, in response to population and business growth.

Your Typical Day

Here are highlights of a typical day for an equipment operator.

✔ **Get your assignment.** You are building a football field with a crew. You arrive at the high school where you are working and find out that your supervisor wants you to spread fill, using a plow and spreader.

✔ **Manage the workload.** Somebody wasn't thinking. The dirt was left behind a pile of gravel, near a fence. You have to create a small roadway before you can start.

✔ **Change gears.** You get a third of the fill down on the ground, but the sky is turning dark with rain clouds—the weather forecast was a little off and you'll have to finish another day. You help get vehicles parked and materials covered. The day ends a bit early, but you know you will be asked to make up time soon.

What You Can Do Now

✯ Get an apprenticeship or part-time employment that introduces you to equipment operation.

✯ Take related vocational and high school classes, such as shop, where you can learn the basics of mechanics, such as how pulleys operate.

✯ Make contacts with people who are in related industries and network.

What Training You'll Need

For some jobs you will be required to show knowledge of basic arithmetic and reading so supervisors know you can follow basic technical directions. Some work in this field will require the use of decimals, fractions, and percentages, especially if you are asked to mix materials.

Much of the expertise is learned on the job. You are watched over and instructed at first in the uses of gauges, dials, and switches and in the powers and dangers of the equipment you will use. You will probably be taught routine maintenance as well, such as oiling the machinery and replacing parts that take the most wear and tear. Then you are allowed to work on your own.

The Inside Scoop: Q&A

Patrick Cale
Crane operator
Fort Wayne, Indiana

Q: *How did you get your job?*

A: I was into [the idea of] running heavy equipment, and I went to an apprenticeship training site and filled out an application, and they accepted me. I went through [several weeks of] training.

Q: *What do you like best about your job?*

A: I love being outdoors, making a pick [lifting other equipment], lifting a piece of equipment up . . . And the people are just fantastic. The other thing is, the things I do will be there forever. I'll be able to point out to my kids, "Hey, I worked on that."

Q: *What's the most challenging part of your job?*

A: You've got to learn what your equipment is going to do and how it's going to work. A lot of what you do takes a lot of coordination. It would be an awfully boring world without challenge, though.

Q: *What are the keys to success to being a manufacturing equipment operator?*

A: Hard work is a definite! Put it all into what you do. Put yourself out there. Always try to make things better.

The progression of training often follows from light machinery to heavy equipment. You are given more trust as you earn it. In many industries formal apprenticeships are available, which lead you from beginner to expert in the use and operation of equipment, such as excavators and graders. Many of these programs are administered by the International Union of Operating Engineers and the Associated General Contractors of America.

No matter where you work, it is quite likely that at some point you will need a commercial driver's license. Even if you do not drive heavy vehicles in a first job, you will likely someday need to be part of a crew of individuals who can cover for one another. So assume that you need to contact your state department of motor vehicles and follow the steps needed for that license. There may be special certifications required of you as well, and they run the gamut. For instance, to operate heavy equipment in the Department of Natural Resources, you need to fulfill the Basic Firefighter Introduction to Fire Behavior course in order to work in their Wildfire Program. Special needs, such as these, will be made clear to you when you apply for open positions.

How to Talk Like a Pro

Here are a few words you'll learn to recognize in this line of work:

- ✴ **Industrial hygiene** This refers to practice of controlling workplace conditions that lead to better safety.
- ✴ **OSHA** The Occupational Safety and Health Administration is the federal agency charged with workplace safety.
- ✴ **Material moving** In this aspect of industry, operators use machinery to move heavy materials. Laborers handle material manually.

How to Find a Job

Jobs are listed in newspaper classified advertisements (online or in print), at employment agencies, and on Web job boards. Pay special attention to the company Web sites of major employers in your area. Often you can check the human resources or employment sections of the sites and find job openings, along with a list of the qualifications the employer seeks. These can be quite specific by machine and vehicle.

Within many industries, you can find formal apprenticeships. Check the Web sites of the International Union of Operating Engineers and the Associated General Contractors of America for more information. But the best way to find employment is to network with people who do the jobs you hope to do. Friends will be the first to tell you when there are openings.

Express your eagerness to begin working. When you are granted an interview, show up on time. Be sure to have all the paperwork you need in order to give your prospective employer contact information for former employers and other references who can speak to your character.

Secrets for Success

See the suggestions below and turn to the appendix for advice on résumés and interviews.

✴ The operator who knows his or her equipment, from design to repair, is the one who gets and keeps good jobs. Be someone who looks beneath the surface.

✴ Without changing jobs too often, make sure you try your hand at as many types of equipment as possible. Being well-rounded means steady employment.

Reality Check

In some jobs, you will be exposed to fumes, loud noises, and dangerous equipment. You have to take safety precautions to protect your hearing, health, and well-being.

Some Other Jobs to Think About

✴ Laboratory technician. You can use your mechanical and technical knowledge in research labs, helping with any number of production and manufacturing projects.

✴ Truck driver. If you are comfortable operating heavy machinery, you may want to take your show on the road—as a professional driver.

✴ Welder. You can use your aptitude for tools to take on all kinds of building and manufacturing functions, such as that of a skilled welder.

How You Can Move Up

✴ Volunteer for an opportunity to lead. As a supervisor, you'll monitor the work of others and maintain related records.

✴ Use what you learn to start your own business.

✴ Teach your skills to others in formal programs.

Web Sites to Surf

International Union of Operating Engineers. You'll find plenty of related information here, including the word on many training programs.
http://www.iuoe.org

Associated General Contractors of America. Information on conferences and issues of the contracting business are covered at this site.
http://www.agc.org

Tackle machinery

Machinist

Give manufacturing problems
an answer

Enjoy creative yet practical
work

Machinist

Machinists make precision parts for machines by cutting and grinding metal. It's meaningful, creative work, yet jobs for machinists outpace the number of people filling them, says CNN.com, in its special online report about jobs expected to experience severe shortages by 2012. Machinists master drills and grinders. They use machining centers and lathes, which shape materials by turning them against a cutting tool. They run milling machines, which cut with rotating teeth. People involved in this line of work solve manufacturing problems by inventing parts.

"You know you're a machinist when you don't return an item that has a missing part," says one machinist on the Internet forum PracticalMachinist.com. "You go out to the shop and make it." That pretty much says it all.

Is This Job for You?

To find out if being a machinist is a good fit for you, answer the following questions with "Yes" or "No."

Yes   No   **1.** Do you like troubleshooting?

Yes   No   **2.** Can you think in basic mathematical terms?

Yes   No   **3.** Are you handy with tools?

Yes   No   **4.** Are you responsible and dependable?

Yes   No   **5.** Are you patient when searching for answers?

Yes   No   **6.** Can you follow directions well?

Yes   No   **7.** Can you read detailed diagrams?

Yes   No   **8.** Are you precise in your work?

Yes   No   **9.** Do you understand the ways that properties define materials?

Yes   No   **10.** Can you see yourself as a craftsperson?

If you answered "Yes" to most of the questions, consider becoming a machinist. To find out more about this job, read on.

What You'll Do

As a machinist, the start of most of your jobs will involve reading specifications and blueprints. After you understand the plans, you'll go into

Let's Talk Money

A starting machinist with computerized numeric control (CNC) skills earned $39,000 as a median salary, and an experienced precision grinder earned a median salary of over $55,000, according to 2006 data from Salary Wizard. Stats for the same year from the U.S. Bureau of Labor Statistics found the mean hourly rate to be nearly $17 and the mean annual salary, nearly $36,000.

planning mode. You have to figure out when to cut into the metal—or whatever the material being molded, from plastic to silicon—how fast to feed the metal into the machinery, and how much metal to remove.

Cutting metal creates a lot of heat, so you must plan for a cooling stage. You also must plan for the finishing of the piece. You'll be marking the piece to show where additional cuts might be made. You'll decide how the cuts will be adjusted as the piece cools.

You then place the metal, for instance, on the correct tool, be it a drill press or a milling machine, and you set the controls so the machine can make the correct cuts. You monitor the speed of the machine and the heat of the material. Most metals expand when heated, so the temperature is important data to track. The other factor that affects metal is vibrations. Those too must be monitored. Otherwise, the precision of the cuts will be off.

Computerized cutting machines now control much of the cutting. The machinist often works with a programmer to determine the path of the cut and the overall speed of the process—or with advanced training, the machinist acts as a programmer himself or herself. Once the piece has been machined, it is checked and measured for quality control. Afterward, machine setters, operators, and tenders finish off the piece. Your careful steps create a machine part that solves a problem in the manufacturing process. When your puzzle is complete, you move on to the next one.

Who You'll Work For

✴ Aerospace product and parts manufacturers
✴ Automobile product and parts manufacturers
✴ Die makers
✴ Millwright shops

Let's Talk Trends

Computers are taking over some machining functions, so eventually fewer workers are going to be needed to do the same work. However, job openings are still predicted to outnumber newly trained machinists.

* Mold-making shops
* Screw, nut, and bolt manufacturers
* Small machine shops
* Subcontractors of all kinds

Where You'll Work

Some machine shops produce large quantities of parts. Others develop small numbers of custom items. So you could be working in a cavernous production shed, filled with robotics, or a small manufacturing site, where fewer machines and workers fill the floors. You'll have space to roam and a place for your tools.

You may be adjacent to manufacturing and finishing floors or off in some kind of shed. But you'll be surrounded by measuring tools, such as calipers, rules, and scales. You'll have electronic measuring tools as well, along with indicators based on clockwork gears. You'll have hand tools and machine tools, though many of the old machine tools have been replaced by computer functions.

On hand will be plenty of raw materials, such as aluminum, brass, copper, and steel. You will probably have glass, rubber, and plastics, as well. And there will be machines of all natures: drills and mills, turners and grinders.

Machinists often stand when they are not immediately involved with their computers. As you work, you'll need to wear protective goggles to keep flying metal out of your eyes. You'll need to put in earplugs to keep machine noise from damaging your hearing.

Your Typical Day

Here are highlights from a typical shift at an aerospace subcontractor.

✓ **Read specifications.** You have been commissioned to create parts for landing gear. You devour related reading materials.

The Inside Scoop: Q&A

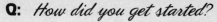

Lewis Heinrichs
Master machinist
Redwood City, California

Q: *How did you get started?*

A: Well, I've been in this trade many, many years, originally just out of high school. I took some classes along the way.

Q: *What do you like best about your job?*

A: Being able to create things! If you enjoy making things, that's quite a lot of the enjoyment of it. And machining jobs are quite stable. If you like to make things and be creative, this is a good job.

Q: *What's the most challenging part of your job?*

A: The big challenge always is running into deadlines. That's probably the stress end of it. But otherwise, this is good work.

Q: *What's your advice for interested students?*

A: Math and computer skills are mainly what you need. The more effort you are giving in trigonometry, the better off you'll be. You need to be able to take something through to an end result. But a lot of things you only develop by getting a job and working.

✓ **Sharpen your tools.** You know a dull machine can spell disaster, so you make the preparations you need.

✓ **Work independently.** You guide a part through the planning, marking, and cutting stages. This part will take you a couple of weeks, with each day bringing you closer to completion.

What You Can Do Now

✯ Take math and computer classes.

✯ Add extra classes like blueprint reading, especially those given at technical and community colleges.

✯ Take work or an apprenticeship working in a shop.

What Training You'll Need

In the new manufacturing age, machining combines automated manufacturing systems and the knowledge and skills wired into the machinist's brain. Getting the training you need is not a one-step process. Machinists need to develop a working understanding of metals and their properties. They need to be handy with tools. So any related part-time work, such as in a fabrication shop, or related schooling, such as blueprint reading at a local community college, can help you get permanent work in this field.

Machinists who can run computerized numeric control (CNC) machines are most valued. So look for classes that give you hands-on experience with CNC machines, or ask for apprenticeship opportunities at a busy shop. Your school should provide you with plenty of practice with bench work, the lathe, milling, and other specialized tools and processes.

You can take this in steps by working first as a machine setter, operator, or tender. Get practice with bench work, the lathe, milling, and other tools of the trade. On the job, you can learn the knowledge you need. You can figure out which classes will help you fill any gaps.

This job requires planning and follow-through. So as far as high school goes, the successful completion of classes like drafting and four years of math will help you prove you have the needed mindset. You read and react to specifications. So pay attention in English classes.

In this line of work, you need to find the best way to create the piece you will need, then mark and cut the material to form, watching for the changes that heat and vibrations make on the metal. Much of this skill will be earned on the job, working under people with more experience, but you can join building clubs and take on projects at home that will show you have the aptitude.

By most measures, the job prospects for future U.S. machinists are quite good. But you can assure your success by looking to facilities that offer curriculum developed by the National Institute of Metalworking Skills. If you pass one of there exams, you'll be well on your way.

How to Talk Like a Pro

Here are a few words you'll use and hear as a machinist:

✯ **Baltimore wrench** This popular tool is a hammer and flat chisel used to remove tight nuts.

✶ **CNC** This stands for computerized numeric control, which reads instructions and drives a machine typically used to fabricate metal components.

✶ **Goldberg** The widely used pet name for any complicated machine, this term came from comics that were drawn by a man by that name and often featured funny, complicated machines.

How to Find a Job

It is wise to seek employment within the field as soon as you can, even taking part-time work while you are still in high school because many of your skills will be developed while you complete real projects that have been assigned to you. Your work as a machinist isn't simply academic; you'll have to put your skills into practice.

A vocational school can provide you with the experience and coursework you need to break into the field as well. Employers who need machinists are often proactive in contacting these schools. You can also, early on, look for apprenticeships available through local labor unions. You can earn points as a go-getter by working as a machine setter, operator, or tender first. It will also put you on an inside track.

When you get an interview, show up on time and be respectful. Have a list of projects you've completed at the ready. Put together a résumé of related classes and job experience.

Secrets for Success

See the suggestions below and turn to the appendix for advice on résumés and interviews.

✶ The difference between success and failure in this line of work is your reverence for quality. Do not settle for "passable."

✶ Become the most computer-literate person in the shop. Highly skilled workers will be first in line to run ever-more-expensive machinery.

Reality Check

You have to be a safety freak to do well in this line of work. Ask any machinist how easy it is to lose a finger!

Some Other Jobs to Think About

✦ Computer control programmer and operator. If you are attracted to this field and are especially adept with computers, you might want to consider taking all the steps needed to program and run related computer equipment.

✦ Tool and die maker. Your skills could also be applied to the field of creating manufacturing forms—for plastics and other materials.

✦ Welder. You can work as a welder or in soldering to be part of the process within that specialization.

How You Can Move Up

✦ Go back for training at intervals throughout your career. New production techniques will call for workers to be jacks-of-all-trades.

✦ Be a take-charge worker. Mentor new machinists. Be dependable and organized. That's how you move into management.

✦ Open your own shop. Eventually, you might want to think about taking on a shop of your own. So pay attention to the ins and outs of the business.

Web Sites to Surf

International Association of Machinists and Aerospace Workers. For a good feel for the concerns of machinists and related unions, go to this site. http://www.goiam.org

National Tooling and Metalworking Association. To find out more about training centers and the kinds of apprenticeship programs that are out there, check out the information given here. http://www.ntma.org

Learn your way around a lab

Chemical Technician

Get behind the scenes of the modern world

Become part of a scientific team

Great Careers

Chemical Technician

Everything breaks into its chemical properties, and in manufacturing, the work of chemical technicians makes up a good part of the success of any operation. Of 325,000 science technicians reporting job stats to the U.S. Bureau of Labor Statistics in 2004, nearly 40 percent of them were in chem tech positions. So if you have taken chemistry and enjoy working in the lab, you might consider a career that keeps you there. Techs help set up and operate lab instruments. They test and help manufacture products. The field encompasses a wide variety of goods, from the plastics that protect stainless steel appliances in transit to hair dye, from food to pharmaceuticals. Anything a chemical engineer works on, a technician works on as well. You could be making detergent. You could be working on fibers used for industrial products. There are all kinds of calls for chemical technicians.

Is This Job for You?

Would working as a chemical technician be a good fit for you? To find out, read the following questions and answer "Yes" or "No."

Yes	No	**1.**	Do you like to analyze ingredients?
Yes	No	**2.**	Are you curious about what makes products work?
Yes	No	**3.**	Are you organized and orderly?
Yes	No	**4.**	Can you multitask?
Yes	No	**5.**	Do you like to work as part of a team?
Yes	No	**6.**	Are you good at following directions?
Yes	No	**7.**	Do you have strong powers of observation—for instance, the ability to see grades of color?
Yes	No	**8.**	Are you good with your hands?
Yes	No	**9.**	Can you remember the properties of various chemicals?
Yes	No	**10.**	Are you a strong communicator, particularly in communicating results?

If you answered "Yes" to most of the questions, you might consider a career as a chemical technician. To find out more about this job, read on.

Let's Talk Money

The median salary for a starting chemical technician ranges from $28,000 to $47,000. That's according to 2007 information from Salary Wizard. The median hourly wage is a little more than $19, or about $41,000 a year, according to 2006 figures from the U.S. Bureau of Labor Statistics.

What **You'll Do**

Technicians work at all stages of manufacturing. The strongest areas of need right now are the biotechnology, environmental, and medical fields, says the American Chemical Society. The best thing about this line of work—hands-down—is its "variety," say the techs who do it.

Starting technicians with high school diplomas work under techs who have more training. Novices are trained to analyze the chemical composition of ingredients and products. They may be looking for purity. They might be making sure the composition is stable. They monitor the lab instruments and log and report data. Sometimes that means preparing charts and diagrams.

This is a hands-on position. You fill and empty pipelines, operate pumps, and turn and test valves. You carefully employ metal and glass tubes and tanks for testing and holding materials. You might be distilling materials or subjecting them to gases. As you gain experience with lab equipment and take more classes, you are given more responsibility. Your firsthand knowledge of the material might be used to plan for material transfer, for instance. In any case, you will keep track of the smallest bits of information. Your powers of observation are called into play.

The increased call for techs in research and development is opening new levels of responsibility to chemical technicians. That, in turn, translates into increased personal rewards. Some technicians test new construction materials or prepare tests for new chemicals in the field. Some specialize in fuel behavior. They test the flash point of fuels—the point at which fuels catch fire. They look for "pour points"—the coldest temperature at which a substance will flow. They also measure heat output.

Let's Talk Trends

Openings for chemical technicians are not expected to grow through 2014, but jobs will become available at a normal rate. Forecasters say the greatest growth will be with firms that sell consumer products, such as pharmaceuticals. Another employment key is the push to create more environmentally friendly products. Consumer and environmental trends make a knowledge or applied science a significant plus in this field.

With this job, you can involve yourself in the application of basic science to supporting the ways of modern life. You will understand the world on the most practical terms, and, no doubt, earn the admiration of family and the appreciation of your employer.

Who You'll Work For

* Beauty supply manufacturers
* Chemical companies
* Environmental companies
* Food producers
* Nuclear energy suppliers
* Petroleum companies
* Pharmaceutical firms
* Plastics manufacturers

Where You'll Work

Let's say you work at a major food corporation in the United States. No day is like another day. Much of your work is carried out within the confines of a laboratory. These are bright, clean, and controlled environments. You will probably have a desk but will undoubtedly be on the go. You might also visit the manufacturing lines, where things are louder and less tame.

You might work around toxic chemicals or even live diseases. There may be breathing hazards. But most employers are careful to protect the people who work for them, as required by law. There will be safety controls working in your favor.

The Inside Scoop: Q&A

Gail L. Parker
Senior technician
Cleveland, Ohio

Q: *How did you get your job?*

A: This goes back to when I graduated from high school. I saw a new plant going up. I went to the old plant and stopped in and asked if they were hiring. I went back every week—every Friday—because I'm a stubborn person.

Q: *What do you like best about your job?*

A: The variety! We have different departments. We work on consumer paints, the Glidden products you'd find under ICI. We take paint formulas, for flat, satin, and semigloss and try different formulas. We try new raw materials and manufacturing techniques.

Q: *What is the most challenging part of your job?*

A: Not enough time! We've downsized in our North American headquarters, and we're in transition. The most challenging thing is trying to do the same amount of work with fewer people.

Q: *What are the keys to success to being a chemical technician?*

A: Everything is going to be "green guarded," you know, environmentally safe. We have to replace everything. So [eventually] a chemical degree or a biology degree [will be needed]. You have to be able to organize your data and present your data. We have book work. You have to know Excel and Word [of the Microsoft Office Suite]. You have to print data and do tables. The key to success is knowing your computer. And we need to get rid of these lazy ideas among American workers because we're so global now. We're outsourcing work.

Techs work in a variety of industries and in governmental or in educational settings. The field is alive with opportunity, especially in biotechnology, computers, energy fields, environmental concerns, materials science, and in quality control. The fact that there is a deep-seated interest in making products that are friendlier to the environment will continue to spur jobs in this field. You might take samples of air pollution, for example. There are many directions you can follow in this field, if you take the needed steps.

Your Typical Day

Here are highlights from a typical shift at a food company.

- ✓ **Hit the floor running.** In food, chemical technicians perform tasks that fall under quality control. Today, you are pulling samples from the line, so you can take them back to the lab and test them for bacteria.
- ✓ **Switch gears.** You meet with a team of techs and scientists to discuss the importance of testing and reporting for a new line of bagged vegetables. People are nervous about the new grade of plastic in the bags and what it might mean in terms of keeping microbes to a minimum.
- ✓ **Write it all down.** You complete paperwork related to the bacteria testing. You fill out assurance reviews that have been developed internally.

What You Can Do Now

- ✴ Take math, chemistry, and other sciences in high school.
- ✴ Look for vocational education that furthers your aim.
- ✴ Apply for an internship or similar program in cooperative education.
- ✴ Take advantage of science competitions and programs.

What Training You'll Need

You need a solid chemistry and math background, so make sure you bulk up on those classes while in high school. Biology classes are well-advised too. Take several years of math and science, along with whatever computer training is available. Taking classes in industrial arts and physics will help round out the bill.

Your mastery of computers will help earn an employer's confidence in you. The other skill that will help you stand out is communications: How well you write and speak and get your ideas across.

Being able to communicate well is a mark of a person who gets ahead, no matter what field. Understanding the importance of business communication is integral in any job.

The main thing you need as a chemical tech, however, is a chemistry background with a manufacturing edge, and that cannot be emphasized too much. Otherwise, you will stay stuck at the entry level, working with plenty of supervision, for years to come. So take whatever chemistry courses are offered in high school and be ready to add to your education at a technical school as time goes on. You'll need to understand methods of analysis and more advanced concepts of chemistry in order to advance yourself.

Remember, there are hardly any industries that have no chemical testing whatsoever. So with advanced education, your skills will translate across the board, and you can find work all over the country. Even while in high school, you can begin to earn extra credits in chemistry in an engineering technology program at a vocational school or community college. Look for computer courses to add to your résumé as well, because computers are integral to the field. Given the rapid advances in key industries, you need to continue your education no matter what. Many firms will help pay for further schooling.

How to Talk Like a Pro

Here are a few technical terms to give you a peek at the work of a chemical technician:

- ✴ **Organic chemistry** This refers to the chemistry of carbon-containing compounds, such as human beings.
- ✴ **R&D** Short for research and development, this is the area that some chem techs find themselves in—for a variety of industries.
- ✴ **GMP** This is short for good manufacturing practice. Federal government regulations define GMP processes. The regulations attempt to maximize safety in the workplace.

How to Find a Job

Your guidance counselor can help you find internships or hook you up with a recruiter. Try to fill a related internship or volunteer position as soon as possible. It shows your seriousness and prepares you for the real challenges of the profession. Join professional associations that can provide the contacts you need. Many also help with internships and summer jobs that help with your résumé.

Any industry or enterprise that involves chemistry hires technicians. You'll find postings on Web job boards and in the classified ads or at employment agencies, including the one run by your state. Look for work at government agencies, in industries, and at universities. You might also find employment with a contractor who brings people in to work in various industries on a project-by-project basis.

For your information, Louisiana and Texas usually pay the highest wages for chemical technicians. Why is that? The area is home to numerous chemical and petroleum companies along the Gulf Coast. Work on offshore oil rigs and at 24-hour refineries pays better than average.

Secrets for Success

See the suggestions below and turn to the appendix for advice on résumés and interviews.

* You can get voluntary certification from the National Institute for Certification in Engineering Technologies, which involves passing an exam, having some job experience, and getting a recommendation. Certification can help you stand out as your career goes along.
* Every job is social—even when you're dealing with test tubes and samples all day long.

Reality Check

Many of these jobs are based on the local needs of specific employers. Without educational enhancement, your skills may not travel as well.

Some Other Jobs to Think About

* Environmental engineering technician. Your interest in chemistry can help in the handling of hazardous materials.
* Quality control technician. If you like the idea of analyzing things, you might consider testing quality at a level other than chemical.

✳ Medical lab technician. You do not have to be limited to lab work in manufacturing. Medical labs need testers of all kinds. Short training programs can land you work in a medical lab.

How You Can Move Up

✳ Decide which industry interests you and get related education beyond chemistry.

✳ Enlist the help of the career placement professionals.

✳ Read related materials from societies of chemists.

✳ Move into management by being dependable and learning all you can on the job.

Web Sites to Surf

American Chemical Society. On this site, there is information on education, industry issues, and much more.   http://www.acs.org

American Chemistry Council. For an overview of chemistry, the economy, and the role of chemistry in daily life, this site is a great place to start. http://www.americanchemistry.org

Unlock your network

Appendix A

Get your résumé ready

Ace your interview

Putting Your Best Foot Forward

When 20-year-old Justin Schulman started job-hunting for a position as a fitness trainer—the first step toward managing a fitness facility—he didn't mess around. "I immediately opened the Yellow Pages and started calling every number listed under health and fitness, inquiring about available positions," he recalls. Schulman's energy and enterprise paid off: He wound up with interviews that led to several offers of part-time work.

Schulman's experience highlights an essential lesson for job seekers: There are plenty of opportunities out there, but jobs won't come to you—especially the career-oriented, well-paying ones that that you'll want to stick with over time. You've got to seek them out.

Uncover Your Interests

Whether you're in high school or bringing home a full-time paycheck, the first step toward landing your ideal job is assessing your interests. You need to figure out what makes you tick. After all, there is a far greater chance that you'll enjoy and succeed in a career that taps into your passions, inclinations, and natural abilities. That's what happened with career-changer Scott Rolfe. He was already 26 when he realized he no longer wanted to work in the food industry. "I'm an avid outdoorsman," Rolfe says, "and I have an appreciation for natural resources that many people take for granted." Rolfe turned his passions into his ideal job as a forestry technician.

If you have a general idea of what your interests are, you're far ahead of the game. You may know that you're cut out for a health care career, for instance, or one in business. You can use a specific volume of Great Careers with a High School Diploma to discover what position to target. If you are unsure of your direction, check out the whole range of volumes to see the scope of jobs available.

You can also use interest inventories and skills-assessment programs to further pinpoint your ideal career. Your school or public librarian or guidance counselor should be able to help you locate such assessments. Web sites, such as America's Career InfoNet (http://www.acinet.org) and Jobweb.com, also offer interest inventories. You'll find suggestions for Web sites related to specific careers at the end of each chapter in any Great Careers with a High School Diploma volume.

Unlock Your Network

The next stop toward landing the perfect job is networking. The word may make you cringe, but networking is simply introducing yourself and exchanging job-related and other information that may prove helpful to one or both of you. That's what Susan Tinker-Muller did. Quite a few years ago, she struck up a conversation with a fellow passenger on her commuter train. Little did she know that the natural interest she expressed in the woman's accounts payable department would lead to news about a job opening there. Tinker-Muller's networking landed her an entry-level position in accounts payable with MTV Networks. She is now the accounts payable administrator.

Tinker-Muller's experience illustrates why networking is so important. Fully 80 percent of openings are *never* advertised, and more than half of all employees land their jobs through networking, according to the U.S. Bureau of Labor Statistics. That's 8 out of 10 jobs that you'll miss if you don't get out there and talk with people. And don't think you can bypass face-to-face conversations by posting your résumé on job sites like Craigslist, Monster.com, and Hotjobs.com and then waiting for employers to contact you. That's so mid-1990s! Back then, tens of thousands, if not millions, of job seekers diligently posted their résumés on scores of sites. Then they sat back and waited . . . and waited . . . and waited. You get the idea. Big job sites have their place, of course, but relying solely on an Internet job search is about as effective throwing your résumé into a black hole.

Begin your networking efforts by making a list of people to talk to: teachers, classmates (and their parents), anyone you've worked with, neighbors, members of your church, synogogue, temple, or mosque, and anyone you've interned or volunteered with. You can also expand your networking opportunities through the student sections of industry associations; attending or volunteering at industry events, association conferences, career fairs; and through job-shadowing. Keep in mind that only rarely will any of the people on your list be in a position to offer you a job. But whether they know it or not, they probably know someone who knows someone who is. That's why your networking goal is not to ask for a job but the name of someone to talk with. Even when you network with an employer, it's wise to say something like, "You may not have any positions available, but would you know someone I could talk with to find out more about what it's like to work in this field?"

Also, keep in mind that networking is a two-way street. For instance, you may be talking with someone who has a job opening that isn't appropriate for you. If you can refer someone else to the employer, either person may well be disposed to help you someday in the future.

Dial-Up Help

Call your contacts directly, rather than e-mail them. (E-mails are too easy for busy people to ignore, even if they don't mean to.) Explain that you're a recent graduate; that Mr. Jones referred you; and that you're wondering if you could stop by for 10 or 15 minutes at your contact's convenience to find out a little more about how the industry works. If you leave this message as a voicemail, note that you'll call back in a few days to follow up. If you reach your contact directly, expect that they'll say they're too busy at the moment to see you. Ask, "Would you mind if I check back in a couple of weeks?" Then jot down a note in your date book or set up a reminder in your computer calendar and call back when it's time. (Repeat this above scenario as needed, until you get a meeting.)

Once you have arranged to talk with someone in person, prep yourself. Scour industry publications for insightful articles; having up-to-date knowledge about industry trends shows your networking contacts that you're dedicated and focused. Then pull together questions about specific employers and suggestions that will set you apart from the job-hunting pack in your field. The more specific your questions (for instance, about one type of certification versus another), the more likely your contact will see you as an "insider," worthy of passing along to a potential employer. At the end of any networking meeting, ask for the name of someone else who might be able to help you further target your search.

Get a Lift

When you meet with a contact in person (as well as when you run into someone fleetingly), you need an "elevator speech." This is a summary of up to two minutes that introduces who you are, as well as your experience and goals. An elevator speech should be short enough to be delivered during an elevator ride with a potential employer from the ground level to a high floor. In it, it's helpful to show that 1) you know the business involved; 2) you know the company; 3) you're qualified (give your work and educational information); and 4) you're goal-oriented, dependable, and hardworking. You'll be surprised how much information you can include in two minutes. Practice this speech in front of a mirror until you have the key points down very well. It should sound natural though, and you should come across as friendly, confident, and assertive. Remember, good eye contact needs to be part of your presentation as well as your everyday approach when meeting prospective employers or leads.

Get Your Résumé Ready

In addition to your elevator speech, another essential job-hunting tool is your résumé. Basically, a résumé is a little snapshot of you in words, reduced to one 8½ x 11-inch sheet of paper (or, at most, two sheets). You need a résumé whether you're in high school, college, or the workforce, and whether you've never held a job or have had many.

At the top of your résumé should be your heading. This is your name, address, phone numbers, and your e-mail address, which can be a sticking point. E-mail addresses such as sillygirl@yahoo.com or drinkingbuddy@hotmail.com won't score you any points. In fact they're a turn-off. So if you dreamed up your address after a night on the town, maybe it's time to upgrade. (And while we're on the subject, these days, potential employers often check Myspace pages, personal blogs, and Web sites. What's posted there has been known to cost candidates job offers.)

The first section of your résumé is a concise Job Objective: "Entry-level agribusiness sales representative seeking a position with a leading dairy cooperative." These days, with word-processing software, it's easy and smart to adapt your job objective to the position for which you're applying. An alternative way to start a résumé, which some recruiters prefer, is to rework the Job Objective into a Professional Summary. A Professional Summary doesn't mention the position you're seeking, but instead focuses on your job strengths: e.g., "Entry-level agribusiness sales rep; strengths include background in feed, fertilizer, and related markets and ability to contribute as a member of a sales team." Which is better? It's your call.

The body of a résumé typically starts with your Job Experience. This is a chronological list of the positions you've held (particularly the ones that will help you land the job you want). Remember: Never, never fudge anything. It is okay, however, to include volunteer positions and internships on the chronological list, as long as they're noted for what they are.

Next comes your Education section. Note: It's acceptable to flip the order of your Education and Job Experience sections if you're still in high school or don't have significant work experience. Summarize any courses you've taken in the job area you're targeting, any certifications you've achieved, relevant computer knowledge, special seminars, or other school-related experience that will distinguish you. Include your grade average if it's more than 3.0. Don't worry if you haven't finished your degree. Simply write that you're currently enrolled in your program (if you are).

In addition to these elements, other sections may include professional organizations you belong to and any work-related achievements, awards, or recognition you've received. Also, you can have a section for your interests, such as playing piano or soccer (and include any notable achievements regarding your interests, for instance, placed third in Midwest Regional Piano Competition). You should also note other special abilities, such as "Fluent in French," or "Designed own Web site." These sorts of activities will reflect well on you whether or not they are job-related.

You can either include your references or simply note, "References Upon Request." Be sure to ask your references permission to use their name, and alert them to the fact that they may be contacted, before you include them on your résumé. For more information on résumé writing, check out Web sites such as http://www.resume.monster.com.

Craft Your Cover Letter

When you apply for a job either online or by mail, it's appropriate to include a cover letter. A cover letter lets you convey extra information about yourself than doesn't fit or isn't always appropriate in your résumé. For instance, in a cover letter, you can and should mention the name of anyone who referred you to the job. You can go into some detail about the reason you're a great match, given the job description. You can also address any questions that might be raised in the potential employer's mind (for instance, a gap in your résumé). Don't, however, ramble on. Your cover letter should stay focused on your goal: to offer a strong, positive impression of yourself and persuade the hiring manager that you're worth an interview. Your cover letter gives you a chance to stand out from the other applicants and sell yourself. In fact, 23 percent of hiring managers say a candidate's ability to relate his or her experience to the job at hand is a top hiring consideration, according to a CareerBuilder.com survey.

You can write a positive, yet concise cover letter in three paragraphs: An introduction containing the specifics of the job you're applying for; a summary of why you're a good fit for the position and what you can do for the company; and a closing with a request for an interview, your contact information, and thanks. Remember to vary the structure and tone of your cover letter. For instance, don't begin every sentence with "I."

Ace Your Interview

Preparation is the key to acing any job interview. This starts with researching the company or organization you're interviewing with. Start with the firm, group, or agency's own Web site. Explore it thoroughly, read about their products and services, their history, and sales and marketing information. Check out their news releases, links that they provide, and read up on, or Google, members of the management team to get an idea of what they may be looking for in their employees.

Sites such as http://www.hoovers.com enable you to research companies across many industries. Trade publications in any industry (such as *Food Industry News*, *Hotel Business*, and *Hospitality Technology*) are also available at online or in hard copy at many college or public libraries. Don't forget to make a phone call to contacts you have in the organization to get a better idea of the company culture.

Preparation goes beyond research, however. It includes practicing answers to common interview questions:

- *Tell me about yourself.* Don't talk about your favorite bands or your personal history; give a brief summary of your background and interest in the particular job area.
- *Why do you want to work here?* Here's where your research into the company comes into play; talk about the firm's strengths and products or services.

⭐ *Why should we hire you?* Now is your chance to sell yourself as a dependable, trustworthy, effective employee.

⭐ *Why did you leave your last job?* Keep your answer short; never bad-mouth a previous employer. You can always say something simple, such as, "It wasn't a good fit, and I was ready for other opportunities."

Rehearse your answers, but don't try to memorize them. Responses that are natural and spontaneous come across better. Trying to memorize exactly what you want to say is likely to both trip you up and make you sound robotic.

As for the actual interview, to break the ice, offer a few pleasant remarks about the day, a photo in the interviewer's office, or something else similar. Then, once the interview gets going, listen closely and answer the questions you're asked, versus making any other point that you want to convey. If you're unsure whether your answer was adequate, simply ask, "Did that answer the question?" Show respect, good energy, and enthusiasm, and be upbeat. Employers are looking for workers who are enjoyable to be around, as well as good workers. Show that you have a positive attitude and can get along well with others by not bragging during the interview, overstating your experience, or giving the appearance of being too self-absorbed. Avoid one-word answers, but at the same time don't blather. If you're faced with a silence after giving your response, pause for a few seconds, and then ask, "Is there anything else you'd like me to add?" Never look at your watch and turn your cell phone off before an interview.

Near the interview's end, the interviewer is likely to ask you if you have any questions. Make sure that you have a few prepared, for instance:

⭐ *"Tell me about the production process."*
⭐ *"What's your biggest short-term challenge?"*
⭐ *"How have recent business trends affected the company?"*
⭐ *"Is there anything else that I can provide you with to help you make your decision?"*
⭐ *"When will you make your hiring decision?"*

During a first interview, never ask questions like, "What's the pay?" "What are the benefits?" or "How much vacation time will I get?"

Find the Right Look

Appropriate dress and grooming is also essential to interviewing success. For business jobs and many other occupations, it's appropriate to come to an interview in a nice (not stuffy) suit. However, different fields have various dress codes. In the music business, for instance, "business casual" reigns for many jobs. This is a slightly modified look, where slacks and a jacket are just fine for a man, and a nice skirt and blouse and jacket or sweater are acceptable for a woman. Dressing overly "cool" will usually backfire.

In general, tend to all the basics from shoes (no sneakers, sandals, or overly high heels) to outfits (no short skirts for women). Women should also avoid attention-getting necklines. Keep jewelry to a minimum. Tattoos and body jewelry are becoming more acceptable, but if you can take out piercings (other than a simple stud in your ear), you're better off. Similarly, unusual hairstyles or colors may bias an employer against you, rightly or wrongly. Make sure your hair is neat and acceptable (consider getting a haircut). Also go light on the makeup, self-tanning products, body scents, and other grooming agents. Don't wear a baseball cap or any other type of hat, and by all means, take off your sunglasses!

Beyond your physical appearance, you already know to be well bathed to minimize odor (leave your home early if you tend to sweat, so you can cool off in private), use a breath mint (especially if you smoke) make good eye contact, smile, speak clearly using proper English (or Spanish), use good posture (don't slouch), offer a firm handshake, and arrive within five minutes of your interview. (If you're unsure of where you're going, Mapquest or Google Map it and consider making a dry run to the site so you won't be late.) First impressions can make or break your interview.

Remember to Follow Up

After your interview, send a thank-you note. This thoughtful gesture will separate you from most of the other candidates. It demonstrates your ability to follow through, and it catches your prospective employer's attention one more time. In a 2005 Careerbuilder.com survey, nearly 15 percent of 650 hiring managers said they wouldn't hire someone who failed to send a thank-you letter after the interview. Thirty-two percent say they would still consider the candidate, but would think less of him or her.

So do you hand write or e-mail the thank you letter? The fact is that format preferences vary. One in four hiring managers prefer to receive a thank-you note in e-mail form only; 19 percent want the e-mail, followed up with a hard copy; 21 percent want a typed hard-copy only, and 23 percent prefer just a handwritten note. (Try to check with an assistant on the format your potential employer prefers). Otherwise, sending an e-mail and a handwritten copy is a safe way to proceed.

Winning an Offer

There are no sweeter words to a job hunter than, "We'd like to hire you." So naturally, when you hear them, you may be tempted to jump at the offer. *Don't.* Once an employer wants you, he or she will usually give you some time to make your decision and get any questions you may have answered. Now is the time to get specific about salary, benefits, and negotiate some of these points. If you haven't already done so, check out salary ranges for your position and area of the country on sites such as Payscale.com, Salary.com, and Salaryexpert.com (basic info is free; specific requests are not). Also find out what sort of benefits similar jobs offer. Then don't be afraid to negotiate in a diplomatic way. Asking for better terms is reasonable and expected. You may worry that asking the employer to bump up his or her offer may jeopardize your job, but handled intelligently, negotiating for yourself may in fact be a way to impress your future employer and get a better deal for yourself.

After you've done all the hard work that successful job-hunting requires, you may be tempted to put your initiative into autodrive. However, the efforts you made to land your job—from clear communication to enthusiasm—are necessary now to pave your way to continued success. As Danielle Little, a human-resources assistant, says, "You must be enthusiastic and take the initiative. There is an urgency to prove yourself and show that you are capable of performing any and all related tasks. If your manager notices that you have potential, you will be given additional responsibilities, which will help advance your career." So do your best work on the job, and build your credibility. Your payoff will be career advancement and increased earnings.

Index